EDITING CORRESPONDENCE

Conference on Editorial Problems

Previous Conference Publications

The Conference volume for 1979 will deal with the editing of illustrated books and will be edited by W.F. Blissett.

Copies of all previous volumes are available through
Garland Publishing Inc.

EDITING CORRESPONDENCE

Papers given at the fourteenth annual
Conference on Editorial Problems,
University of Toronto,
3–4 November 1978

EDITED BY J.A. DAINARD

Garland Publishing, Inc., New York & London

1979

Copyright © 1979

by

The Conference on Editorial Problems

All rights Reserved

Library of Congress Cataloging in Publication Data

Conference on Editorial Problems, 14th, University
of Toronto, 1978.
 Editing correspondence.

 Includes index.
  1. Editing--Congresses.   2. Letters--Congresses.
I. Dainard, J.A. II. Title
PN162.C62 1978   801'.956   79-11603
ISBN 0-8240-2429-X

Printed in the United States of America

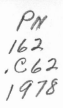

Contents

Notes on Contributors

ALAN BELL is an Assistant Keeper in the Department of Manuscripts at the National Library of Scotland. He is Secretary of the Survey of the Letters of Sir Walter Scott, and was in charge of the books and manuscripts section of the Sir Walter Scott Bicentenary Exhibition (1971). He has contributed book reviews on modern literary and biographical subjects to the *Times Literary Supplement* and other journals. He is the author of a forthcoming biography of Sydney Smith, and is working on a four-volume revised edition of *The Letters of Sydney Smith,* both to be published by Oxford University Press. He edited the *Scott Bicentenary Essays* (1971) and *Sir Leslie Stephen's Mausoleum Book* (1977).

ROBERT FINCH is Emeritus Professor of French at the University of Toronto, and a Senior Fellow of Massey College.

He is author of *The Sixth Sense: Individualism in French Poetry, 1686-1760* (1966), and co-editor with Eugène Joliat of *French Individualist Poetry, 1686-1760, an Anthology* (1971), and of Saint-Evremond's *Sir Politick Would-Be* (1978) and *Les Opéra* (in press). His volumes of verse include *Acis in Oxford* (1961) and *Silverthorn Bush* (1966).

RALPH A. LEIGH is Professor of French at the University of Cambridge and Professorial Fellow of Trinity College, Cambridge. He is editor of the *Correspondance complète de Jean-Jacques Rousseau*, which began to appear in 1965, and is author of numerous articles on eighteenth-century French literature. He is currently working on a bibliography of editions of Rousseau's writings.

WILMARTH S. LEWIS, author, collector, editor and lecturer, is editor of *The Yale Edition of Horace Walpole's Correspondence*, which began to appear in 1937, and will soon number more than forty volumes. His many books and articles include *Collector's Progress* (1951), *Horace Walpole* (1961), *One Man's Education* (1968), and *Rescuing Horace Walpole* (1978).

JOHN MATTHEWS is Professor of English at Queen's University, Kingston. He is the author of *Tradition in Exile* (1962), and of articles and essays on Canadian literature and Canadian writers. Since its inception in 1973, he has been Senior Editor and Principal Investigator of the Disraeli Project. The first two volumes of Disraeli's correspondence are to appear in 1979.

JOHN A. WALKER is Professor of French at the University of Toronto. He is author of articles and book-reviews on French literature of the sixteenth and nineteenth centuries. He is General Secretary of the Zola Programme, and one of the contributing editors; the first volume of Zola's *Correspondance* appeared in 1978.

EDITING CORRESPONDENCE

Introduction

J.A. Dainard

The fourteenth annual Conference on Editorial Problems was held November 3 and 4, 1978, on the campus of the University of Toronto. The topic was "Editing Correspondence," and five papers were given. The first was read on Friday evening by Wilmarth S. Lewis, on the editing of letters in general. On Saturday morning, Alan Bell spoke on Sir Walter Scott's letters, and Ralph Leigh on his edition of Rousseau's correspondence; in the afternoon, John A. Walker spoke on the editing of Zola's letters, and John Matthews on his work on Disraeli's correspondence. The range of subjects represented English and French writers of the eighteenth and nineteenth centuries, including one chiefly non-literary figure, Disraeli. All of the projects with which the speakers are associated are large ones, and the speakers themselves represent editors with varying degrees of experience. Three of the enterprises are team projects: the Walpole edition now is nearing completion after forty-five productive years; the Disraeli and Zola editions, both supported by the Social Sciences and Humanities Research Council of Canada, are now publishing their first volumes - and we are told that further volumes will henceforth be appearing in relatively quick succession. Ralph Leigh's edition of Rousseau, on the other hand, is a one-man venture: the first volume appeared in 1965, thirty-five volumes have appeared at the present time, and completion of the edition, in some forty volumes, is foreseen for the early 1980s. The Scott project is still undergoing the interesting process of definition.

It is clear, from examining the interests of the delegates to the Conference (their attendance established a record), that the business of editing correspondence is flourishing. The convenor had realized this long ago, when trying to plan a broad but coherent programme within the limits of the traditional five papers; there seemed an almost unlimited choice of highly competent editors, young and old. The writers being investigated by the delegates to this Conference alone present a broad spectrum. These letter-writers include, from the British Isles: Eduard Bertz, Dr. Charles Burney, Fanny Burney, Thomas Carlyle, Lord Chesterfield, William Cowper, George Gissing, Edmund Gosse, Thomas Hardy, Constance Holme, Charles and Mary Lamb, D.H. Lawrence, Austin Henry Layard, Macaulay, Mark Pattison, Bertrand Russell, Sydney Smith, W.B. Yeats; from France: Diderot, Etienne Falconet, Madame de Graffigny, Claude-Adrien Helvétius, André Morellet, Eugène Scribe; from Canada: William Arthur Deacon and Arthur Stringer; and from the United States: Henry Adams, Isabella Eliza Hart, Bret Harte, Nathaniel Hawthorne, John Hay, and William Dean Howells. One delegate is working on the correspondence of several Victorian novelists with their French publisher, Hachette; and another is preparing an anthology of English familiar letters of the seventeenth century. It was an attentive and committed audience, therefore, which the speakers had before them.

Although the five papers differed in subject and perspective and emphasis, certain motifs kept recurring. Among the most persistent was the conviction with which all speakers affirmed the usefulness of editions of private letters. Their interest is not only biographical, but also historical, social, artistic, and literary. The letters are an extension of the author's formal writings, and an elucidation of the public and private man. The editor's commitment to the man and to the expression of his private thoughts and actions imposes the responsibility of presentation of a complete and accurate text, for both the casual reader and the scholarly researcher. Almost all of the speakers found themselves obliged to improve on previous editions, which were found unsatisfactory for a variety of reasons. The main problems in the new edition are to gather together the texts, to establish the text, and to comment on the text, to "faire vivre une correspondance et la rendre parlante."[1] This commitment to the writer and to his readers was strongly asserted by all speakers. Another theme, implicit or explicit, was not to take anything for granted: everything must be checked, no matter how eminent the earlier editors, no matter how inaccessible the manuscripts, no matter how authoritative the reference work. The editor must aim, as Mr. Lewis states, at complete understanding. That all the speakers felt this no doubt accounts for the sense of drama and excitement which animated all the papers.

Wilmarth Lewis graciously and courageously made the trip

---

1 / Georges Lubin, *Les Editions de Correspondances: colloque du 20 avril 1968*, Paris, Colin, 1969, p. 91. Other such conferences are reported in "Les Correspondances, leur importance pour l'histoire des sciences et de la philosophie, Journées de Chantilly, 5-7 mai 1975," *Revue de Synthèse*, no. 81-82, 97 (1976), 1-189; and *Probleme der Brief-Edition*, Kolloquium der Deutschen Forschungsgemeinschaft, 8-11 September 1975, Boppard, Harald Bolt, 1977.

to Toronto to deliver his sound advice to both novice and experienced editors, for which he received the tribute of a standing ovation. Editing, he observes, is the least studied and respected of scholarly exercises; in the absence of the manual on editing correspondence promised before his death by Jean Bonnerot, Sainte-Beuve's editor, but unfortunately never written, the delegates had in Mr. Lewis's address the combination of inspiration, wit, and practical common sense which only long experience and judicious insight can provide. Professor Leigh, bravely consenting to deliver yet one more address as his heavy Rousseau Bicentenary drew to a close, dwells, with elegant concision, on problems peculiar to the Rousseau letters, and the way in which they determine the textual features of his edition. The result is a model that is being closely followed by other editors of eighteenth-century French correspondences. Alan Bell, contributing the special perspective of the archivist, describes the unique problems of the Scott correspondence, tells of the project now in progress, and, in speculating on what the future might hold, gives precious information for all those on the threshold of large-scale enterprises. John Walker, while treating in detail one problem which besets most editors, gives insight into the Zola edition's processes as a whole, and a rich over-view of important recent editions of nineteenth-century France. John Matthews dwells on a theme only touched on by earlier speakers, that of the hunt for manuscripts: the Disraeli letters presented unique problems, and also familiar ones. He concludes by challenging incipient editors to exploit untapped resources, such as those which he found while looking for Disraeli letters.

The Committee of the Conference on Editorial Problems extends its thanks to the Social Sciences and Humanities Research Council of Canada for its generous support, and to the University of Toronto for sponsoring the Conference. Thanks for financial aid go also to the Department of English, the Department of French, and the Office of the Dean of the Faculty of Arts and Science. Special thanks go to Robert Finch for so eloquently and amusingly welcoming the delegates in verse, and for consenting to have his *discours en vers* included in this volume. As convenor of the 1978 Conference, I should like to express my personal thanks to the other members of the Conference Committee, especially Angus Cameron, Hugo de Quehen, Robin Jackson, Richard Landon, Jane Millgate, and Desmond Neill; to Professors D.I.B. Smith, Thomas Pinney, D.W. Smith, B.H. Bakker, and G.E. Bentley, Jr., for so ably chairing the sessions of the Conference; to Mary Garvie Yohn and Richard Landon for mounting in the Thomas Fisher Rare Book Library a special exhibition, and producing the accompanying catalogue entitled "Letters as Literature"; to Carolynn Jackson for setting the text and to Cameron Louis for proofreading this volume.

Welcoming Address

Robert Finch

Ladies and gentlemen, I begin with an acrostic on the word

CORRESPONDENCE

Colleagues and friends, it is for me an honour,
Of course, to welcome you, as I now do.
Recommendations that my words be few
Rush to my mind. I shall, to finish sooner,
Exert my feeble talents to augment
Salutations from University
Plus Massey with brief verses that will be
On themes more or less keyed to this event,
Neglected themes yet relevant to your own,

Dedicated to you, for your diversion,
Easy of access, easier of dispersion,
None the less made for you and you alone;
Correspondence evoked what they compile,
Editors, would they were worthier your while.

I now offer a concise history of correspondence.

1

Correspondence, which dates from the deluge, is
Itself a deluge, cuneiform, papyrus,
Parchment. Paper, the latest to inspire us
As writers of letters, has long been hers and his,
Yet paper came from China very late,
The earliest known European screed
On paper is a deed of Adélaïde,
Countess of Sicily, with the unlooked-for date
Eleven hundred and two, and from that missive
It was to prove a far cry to the time
When postal figures would begin to climb
Up to the point at which your work grows massive,
When poetry and novels start to yield
To a new rival in the graphic field.

2

It is then that the expression 'correspondence'
Meaning communication held by letters
And the letters themselves, sent and received by writers,
Begins to be used by the latter in abundance.
It appears at the same time in England and in France,
At the 17th century's middle, and thenceforth
The new concept to new concepts gives birth:
'Education advances, correspondence must advance';

'Letters should be free and easy as one's chatter,
Not studied orations, nor studded with hard words';
'Remember that pens are mightier than swords';
'Let your letter stay for the post, not the post for the letter';
And, since letter-writing loathes the least abscondence,
'Letter for letter is the law of correspondence'.

3

No wonder your job became constantly greater and greater,
As writers of letters accepted such advice.
Then voices began to dub the virtue vice:
'The postscript is the pith of a woman's letter';
'We hardly learn to ply the pen than thought
And fancy faint with cold'. 'Better to live
Under misrepresentation than to give
Uncertain light no letter ever caught'.
'Correspondence may be compared to breeches
Before the innovation of suspenders.
Impossible to keep them up'. Do senders
And do receivers heed the voice that preaches?
The more the art of letters is forbidden,
The more the attic trunks grow letter-ridden.

So the art of letters suffers neither from enthusiasm nor from
denigration. But are there not other dangers? What about
postal service?

1

Postal service begins with the ark's dove,
Who brings those olive leaflets telling peace
Is re-established over floods that cease
To swell and rage below, between, above.
While useless to perform in weather Stygian,

On a clear day a pigeon has the power
Of thirty-five to ninety miles an hour.
No postman is more faithful than the pigeon.
Though time and time again pigeons were ousted
By every other system known to man,
Foot, horse, coach, train or steel-winged maxi-plane,
We yet look for the day when letters posted,
At any season, radiant or dark,
May reach us as those leaflets reached the ark.

2

That wish is not an idle one to make,
Next spring, they promise, it will be fulfilled,
Then letters electronically mailed
Will take less time than present letters take.
Your message, sliced to snips of information,
Some hand will feed up to a satellite
Which carries them to where, when they alight,
Microwaves waft them to the postal station;
There back to letter-form they are revised
By yet another hand; next, probably,
A further hand will do delivery,
By courier-service yet to be devised.
We must admit one never saw the like —
Though couriers, conceivably, could strike . . .

3

Strikes or no strikes, will letters still survive
Or have they had their almost final say?
Lord Chesterfield, Madame de Sévigné,
Walpole, Sainte-Beuve, etcetera, are alive,
But think of a future Sydney Smith, a Gide,
Pouring his soul out for a satellite

To cut in bits the P.O. will re-write,
Why, it would kill the letter-writing breed!
'A single form per letter. Kindly file
Your carbon copy. Type, so we can read it'.
The standard electronic letter-style
Will leave you people less and less to edit.
'Use one side only, keep to the dotted lines.
Infractions will be liable to fines'.

The preparation of letters for electronic circulation may well
do away with handwriting. So let us look at this now uncon-
sidered and all-but-lost feature of correspondence.

1

A handsome hand we call calligraphy,
An illegible one is known as sparrow-tracks,
All else beside those counter whites-and-blacks
We label writing indiscriminately.
Whatever the script, letters are two-faced babblers.
All scribes let pen and ink lay bare their fate,
Forgetting the very thing they most would hate,
That writing, good or bad, depicts its scribblers.
Yes, as the pen turns, everything turns clear,
What the words do not say, their shape unseals,
What the words try to hide, their form reveals,
Reading between the lines comes nowhere near.
The altering of chirographic manner
From an analysis protects no penner.

2

A letter may be plain as plain in tone,
Full of city, country, art, news, poetry,
Sport, business, pleasure, children, family,

Nothing the writer would prefer unknown.
Yet find a haruspex, he will set free
The innards of your writing and will scan
The entrails of that script as no one can,
The things that were, that are and that shall be,
Your life's events, your very mind's recesses,
He will unfold, your past and future woes
And joys, for certain, not with fanciful guesses,
Since as the heavens go your writing goes.
The pattern of your syllables refers
To you and to the pattern of your stars.

3

Though letters may not show when they were penned,
Nor from what place nor even yet to whom,
And bear no name, always their hand leaves room
For speculation, which may never end.

A letter that is printed must omit
What is in fact the heart and soul of it,
But a hand-written letter points the way
To spy the needle hidden in its hay.

Once symbols came from whirly queues of birds,
They find them now in curlecues of words;
By 'they' are meant those maybe here now present,
Those experts to haruspicate equipped,
Who edit letters left in manuscript,
Not for what is expressed but for what isn't.

All the same, whether a letter is written or printed or typed
or computerized, it will still be a letter, with, at the very least,
a letter's two most fascinating problems.

A letter is a photo of the writer
As he would be remembered in the eyes
Of the receiver, whether or not he tries.
And snapped among the traits of the inditer
Are traits of the receiver; these, though slighter,
Are there, for your trained glance to recognize
And from that double likeness to surmise
Whether the bonds grow looser or pull tighter.
True for each letter, but when all find places
Inside one album, how construe their range?
What candour has a camera that can change
One face into so many different faces?
Where in this crowd of portraits is *le vrai*?
And which receiver least got in the way?

Some of you may well wonder why my remarks have mainly
preferred the sonnet form. There are two reasons. Here is
the first:

A sonnet is the ideal letter still;
Addressed to one, all are addressed by it;
Neither too short nor long, it has to fit
Within a space not more or less would fill.
It has one subject, plus the reason why,
And each directs the other's pantomime,
The subject springs with reason into rhyme
Which reason springs with wit to justify.
It reaches a conclusion on its own,
Asks for no answer, knowing none will come,
Is both its carrier and delivery,
A sonnet is a letter cut in stone,
Light as a snowflake, vibrant as a drum,
And posted in the air, content to die.

Here is the second reason. I observed that this is the fourteenth annual Conference on Editorial Problems, and that there are fourteen letters in 'correspondence'. If someone also wonders why I did not make fourteen sonnets, it is because I promised your convenor that my speaking time should not exceed fourteen minutes.

Editing Familiar Letters

Wilmarth S. Lewis

The new edition of Horace Walpole's letters was first proposed at the Modern Language Association meeting in December 1932. I pointed out three reasons for it: to correct the text, to annotate it fully, and to print the letters to Walpole. I also pointed out that Walpole lived for nearly eighty years at the centre of affairs, and wrote the history of his time in his letters with us, posterity, in mind. Whatever the subject, I said - tar water or the elder Pitt's gout, Mrs. Delany's paper flowers or the conquest of Canada - you will find it in his letters. My proposed edition would be an encyclopaedia of the eighteenth century. When I finished there was an uneasy silence that was broken by a humorist who asked me to read some of the expurgated passages I had recovered. A titter ran round the room. Fortunately, Yale took the project more seriously, and on the first of July, 1933, Dayle Wallace, who had just got his Ph.D. under Chauncey Tinker, began work as my assistant on the Yale edition of Horace Walpole's correspondence in the new Sterling Memorial Library. Now, forty-five years later, our forty-eight volumes are almost finished. They could not have been done without the contributions of many colleagues at Yale presided over by Warren Hunting Smith, who edited the seventeen volumes of the du Deffand and Mann correspondences and produced our index of a million entries in six volumes.

The editor of private letters is waved on his way by Horace Walpole himself, who wrote, "Nothing gives so just an idea of an age as genuine letters; nay, history waits for its last seal from them." "But how," a fledgling editor may ask, "do I begin?" The answer is, "Find the originals of the letters you are going to edit, the published as well as the unpublished." Until you see the manuscripts, you cannot be certain you have what your author wrote. Since your predecessors seldom collated their proofs with the originals, their errors of transcription went uncorrected as the new editor added errors of his own.

Earlier editors "improved" their texts. Mason cut and spliced Gray's letters. Miss Berry gouged out proper names in Walpole's letters, suppressed passages that might be objectionable, and laid the soft hand of refinement upon Rabelaisian jokes. Being a writer herself with views about what was interesting and what was not, she crossed out whole paragraphs.

An author's family tends to protect him. If it discovers that grandfather, the great poet, corresponded ardently with an opera singer in Milan, his letters to her may be burnt and the scholars frustrated who suspect that the "Laura" of his sonnets was more than a disembodied spirit. Families can be conscienceless. A woman wrote Mrs. Paget Toynbee, "There was among my dear aunt's papers a roll marked H. More. I fetched it up one day and tried to decipher a few, but they came to pieces in my hands and I demolished them forthwith

. . . There were several, I think, of H. Walpole's, but I have such a horror of accumulating relics."

The surviving letters are in bookshops, libraries, and private hands, in that order of accessibility. Dr. Rosenbach allowed scholars to print his unpublished letters, but many booksellers refuse to do so in the belief that publication lessens their commercial value, a debatable point.

Manuscripts in libraries may be hard to find. When I began the Yale Walpole forty-five years ago, I sent a circular letter announcing the project to eight hundred libraries round the world asking them if they had any letters to or from Walpole and hoping that they would let me print them if they had. I did this on the urging of a veteran librarian. Only eight of the eight hundred replied, yet one, the National Library of Victoria at Melbourne sent me a photostat of an unpublished letter in its possession. Eight replies and a brand new letter, I realize now, was not too bad for eight hundred circular letters. Friends, including several librarians, have found for me hundreds of letters in the libraries I wrote to. Friends discover more than circular letters.

Private owners who have inherited their letters may not know what they have, but they usually want to be helpful. Their patience is tried when the editor assumes he has a right to their private property because it is "his" man's manuscripts, or if he is insensitive to the trouble and perhaps expense he is putting the owners to.

At the outset you know where a certain number of the manuscripts are, thanks to your predecessors' and your own researches. You also know that many of your man's letters were destroyed by their recipients. How does one find the survivors? The new editor usually announces his project in the *Times Literary Supplement* and requests the use of the letters in its readers' possession. He awaits eagerly the harvest of new material, but when my announcement appeared in the *TLS* I didn't get one reply.

Nor have I had any success with wills. Walpole directed that all the letters to him that he had kept should be returned to their writers on his death if they survived him. A professional searcher of wills went to work for me at Somerset House to trace Walpole's vast correspondence with his sister, Lady Mary Churchill, who outlived him. Lady Mary had a large family, all of whom were equally fruitful. They became an army that followed the flag round the earth. Grandchildren went to India, great-grandchildren to New Zealand; heaven knows where the great-great-grandchildren got to, for we gave up when we reached them. Then I happened to meet one of Lady Mary's descendants. "Oh yes," she said, "I know all about Horace Walpole's letters to Lady Mary Churchill. They belonged to my Uncle George in Dorset."

"And your Uncle George?" I asked.

"My Uncle George went mad during the War and believed the Germans were about to land near him to seize his papers. To frustrate them he threw the lot into the fire, shouting with laughter."

I failed to find a letter to or from Walpole through Somerset House, but in the catalogues of London and New York auctioneers I've found some 1,600. Even if the catalogues don't lead you to the letters themselves, they may give you extracts from unpublished letters.

It is wise to make friends with the government officials who examine country house libraries for probate. If you are squeamish about being a ghoul, don't think of becoming an editor. Your spirit must hover over stately homes long before their owners are borne away to the family vault. You can't afford not to be in the minds of survivors.

The editor must expose himself to chance. During the War I saw something of a genial Englishman who was in line to inherit a famous country house. When I asked him my usual question, he said he was afraid his family had no Walpoliana. The only thing of value they had was furniture. There they'd had a bit of luck. When the house was built, the estate carpenter who made the new chairs and tables and carved the overmantels was a chap named Thomas Chippendale. In due course my friend succeeded to the property and another friend who probated the contents of the house found twenty-three unpublished letters to Horace Walpole about his *Historic Doubts of Richard III.* Six of them belonged in a correspondence being printed at that moment in the Yale Walpole. The new owner kindly rushed the letters to the British Museum to be photostated, and they reached the Yale University Press just in time to be fitted into their proper places.

The editor may try broadcasting, magazine articles, and advertising. I have had little success with the first two. A national broadcast in Australia brought me many letters, but none from or to Horace Walpole. One broadcast on the Third Programme of the B.B.C. revealed two Walpole letters in Geneva; two other broadcasts on the same programme turned up no letters, but did produce two chairs from Strawberry Hill. Magazine articles have brought one letter, advertising in the Agony Column of the *London Times* over five hundred.

Besides these steps is what Walpole called Serendipity, a word he invented to describe finding something while looking for something else. By Serendipity we have chanced upon many letters to and from Walpole that were printed in out-of-the-way places. There have also been the occult occasions when I have seen a shop glowing with a mysterious light and found in it a letter to or from Walpole or a book from the Strawberry Hill library. I have astonished librarians by taking off their shelves books from Walpole's library that neither they nor I knew were in the building. This sort of thing does not astonish collectors and editors.

The new editor must devise a filing and cataloguing system for his letters and the materials relating to them. His system should be better than the one used by the first editor of Walpole's 450 letters to Lady Ossory. The family kept them tied up year by year with corset strings that cut into the letters. After the editor finished 1777, he skipped to 1779, and eighty-seven years went by before it was discovered that he had overlooked thirty-one superb letters of 1778 and nineteen others. This carelessness was common when letter-writing was regarded as a genteel pastime and letters were edited, in Walpole's phrase, "with all the beautiful negligence of a gentleman." It is otherwise now when we have the photographic processes developed by the most successful agency of research the world has ever known, big business. Of course, no system is fool-proof, as I learned when I found a new letter to Walpole belonging in a correspondence we had already published, for I owned that letter when we edited that correspondence.

There are three questions the new editor must answer at the outset: "Shall I print all the letters of my man or only those I consider 'interesting'? Shall I print the letters *to* my man? Shall I publish chronologically or by correspondences?"

If you decide to print only the letters you consider interesting, you will have to weigh and balance each case, now admitting, now rejecting, for reasons that may differ from day to day. If you would earn for your edition the most fleeting of academic adjectives, "definitive," you must print all. Even if the letters *to* your man double the size of your edition, they will not double your labours, because the letters to him will answer many questions raised by the letters from him. Without the correspondents' replies, the reader is like a person hearing only one side of a telephone conversation. The other side may have its own importance. The Yale Walpole is enriched by the letters from Mme du Deffand and Gray. Your decision to publish chronologically or by correspondences will depend on the bulk of the entire body of letters and on their nature, on whether the separate correspondences are large enough to have an entity of their own that would be destroyed by the intrusion of other letters, or whether the chronological flow, which gives a conspectus of your author's life, is of paramount importance.

Let us now suppose you are ready to begin annotating the letters from the original manuscripts, copies, photostats, microfilm, or the best printed text. You start to transcribe the letters - and encounter immediately four editorial problems.

The thorniest of them is in the first sentence you transcribe. Are you going to modernize your man's spelling, punctuation, etc.? (Whatever you do will annoy those who believe you should have done the opposite.) The next three problems are identifying the unknown correspondents, dating undated letters, and deciphering illegible words and passages. These problems are less difficult than they might seem to be. Out of the 7,000-odd letters in the Yale Walpole, only sixty are to or from unidentified correspondents, and there are only a similar number of undated letters. As to illegibility, even the most difficult hand eases in time. What may be impossible are mutilations. Heavy overscorings made with the same ink (presumably by the original writer) may accomplish the deletor's purpose; if the two inks are different, infra-red may reveal the erased words. When an earlier owner has cut out a passage with shears, something may be guessed from the ascenders and descenders that have survived, but, if the page went into the fire you can only pray that a copy of it will turn up.

You type the letters with one carbon. The fair copy is put aside to the far-distant day when it receives the super-numbers for the notes before it is sent to the printer. The notes are written on separate sheets from which the editor makes a working index of proper names. This is not the final analytical index that will fill five or six stout volumes in the Yale Walpole with a million entries. The working index establishes the *dramatis personae* in your head at the outset and gets the entire correspondence before you.

Thanks to the Anglo-Saxon passion for self-documentation, members of the clergy, of Parliament, of the armed forces, alumni of universities, usually present no difficulty. The "Linen Draper, at the Old Black Boy, in Norton Folgate," is a challenge, but tradesmen's directories and collections of tradesmen's cards may produce him. Occasionally you will have to give up. We have been beaten by a Twickenham neighbour of Walpole's, "a strange foolish woman that lives at the great corner house yonder; she is an attorney's wife, and much given to her bottle; by the time she has finished that and daylight she grows afraid of thieves and makes her servants fire minute guns out of the garret windows." You would suppose this lady could be identified without too much trouble, but she has eluded us for forty years because the English have yet to compile a directory of attorney's wives who have taken to the bottle.

Before you begin to explicate the text, you must decide whether you are going to number the letters, how you will head them, and where you are giving the present owner of the letter and its history. Where will you put its address and postmark (if any) and the memoranda that may be on it? And having decided these preliminaries, what "style" will you adopt for your notes? Publishing houses have their own style books, all of which differ from each other. You will find helpful points in most of them, but will begin waking up in the middle of the night wondering what on earth is the difference between *ibid* and *idem* (or *ib.* and *id.*), and how should you handle that firefly of the scholarly swamps, *cf.*? When you have answered these questions, you must decide whether you will print the constricted Latin adverbs in Roman or italic. You will be wise to make your own style book, of which you will become fond; in fact, you must guard against becoming too fond of it. Resist the temptation to invent ingenious devices for presenting your notes and index. Do not on any account be clever. References should be made in as concise a manner as possible, but compression can be carried too far; the edition should not be turned into a private language intelligible only to those initiated into it. "Lucidity, simplicity, system," were recommended by Sir Henry Maine.

Now at last you have reached the point where you begin to elucidate the text; now you are on your own, just as Alice was when she started across the chessboard and the Red Queen advised her, "Speak in French when you can't think of the English for a thing, turn out your toes as you walk, and remember who you are." With a similar desire to be helpful, I would advise the editor at the outset of his long journey: "Keep to the middle of the road, don't show off, and look out for hypertension."

The middle of the road between those who are resolved to be "thorough," whatever that means, and the lazy, who believe that the reader can do a good deal of the work himself, is not always easy to find. Editors who point out all the steps they have taken to solve a problem, the learned works they consulted that were of no use to them, and the errors of those ludicrous fumblers, their predecessors, are not admired. Nor will the reader want references to works printed at Magnetogorsk or Rondebosch if they have appeared in London or New York. It is a mistake for an editor to display his ingenuity, mastery of libraries, and indomitable will.

The causes of hypertension lurk everywhere. There is the fear of missing an obvious reference and being called "superficial"; there is the annoyance of having "new" letters turn up after the edition is published. Although editing is perhaps the least studied and respected of scholarly exercises, it is one of the most useful, and an editor may be subject to the gusts of self-pity that upset unappreciated people aware of their own merit.

As editor you should follow two rules. The first is, Do What is Best for the Reader, who doubtless shares with you common knowledge. This means you should probably elucidate those passages and references you didn't understand when you first read them, and that you may leave what was clear alone. Therefore you do not give the *loci* of "To be or not to be" or *"Arma virumque cano,"* nor need you identify Jupiter, Juno, or Potiphar's wife, but your reader probably won't snap at you if you remind him where he can find "Patriotism is the last refuge of a scoundrel," or who Galatea was. It is often best for the editor to do nothing. When Walpole wrote from France that the French had become very simple in their dress and equipages, that the English were living upon their old gods and goddesses, and that "I roll about Paris in a chariot decorated with Cupids and look like the grandfather of Adonis," we didn't intrude with a note on Adonis or his grandfather. Nor do I think editorial help is needed with this passage in a letter to Lady Ossory: "When by the aid of some historic vision and local circumstance I can romance myself into pleasure, I know nothing transports me so much . . . I sometimes dream, that one day or other, somebody will stroll about poor Strawberry and talk of Lady Ossory - but alas! I am no poet, and my castle is paper, and my castle and my attachment and I shall soon vanish and be forgotten together!" It would be a disservice to the reader, I think, to point out that Walpole was the author of x-1,000 lines of verse, that instead of vanishing soon he lived nineteen years, six months, and sixteen days longer, that Strawberry Hill is still standing two hundred years later in spite of the encroachments of Greater London and a German bomb on the night of 14 December 1941 and that Walpole himself, far from being forgotten, is one of the best-known men of his age.

The second inflexible rule of editing is Don't Annotate the Annotation. If the editor does so, his notes will get longer and longer until they overflow into appendices, into monographs, and swell into a super-colossal work no publisher in his right mind would publish. The editor will have unleashed a bag of winds that will blow him and his work into oblivion, to everybody's enormous relief.

"It is impossible," said Dr. Johnson, "for an expositor not to write too little for some, and too much for others. He can only judge what is necessary by his own experience; and how longsoever he may deliberate, will at last explain too many lines which the learned will think impossible to be mistaken, and omit many for which the ignorant will want his help. These are censures merely relative, and must be quietly endured."

The editor rises above routine footnotes when he adds pertinent unprinted material, such as contemporary evidence that proves or disproves his man's statements. An example of what I mean is found in William Cole's copy of *A Description of Strawberry Hill.* Cole wrote in a margin that Conyers Middleton complained to him of Walpole's paying him only £20 for his fine collection of classical antiquities. Cole is dependable; we believe he understood Middleton to say Walpole paid him only £20 for his collection. Left at that, Walpole appears as a rich young man who defrauded an old scholar to whom he owed much. Yet in one of his copies of *A Description of Strawberry Hill* at Farmington, Walpole noted that he paid Middleton £125 for his collection. Who was right, Cole or Walpole? The question is settled by the receipt for the transaction, signed by both Middleton and Walpole, which is also at Farmington. This proves that Walpole gave Middleton not £20, not £125, but 125 guineas. Producing such proof whenever he can is certainly part of an editor's job, but having produced it, he must resist the temptation to pursue the question of Middleton's statement. So great an error is hard to explain. Middleton had urged Walpole to ask his father to make him a bishop. Walpole did so without success. By reducing the handsome sum that Walpole gave him to a contemptible one, was Middleton paying off a grudge? The editor may wonder and speculate, but he must not put his lucubrations into a note, because that would be annotating the annotation. He must not try to write all the books his edition will inspire.

We editors have knowledge that the letter-writers and his friends lacked. We know the joys and sorrows in store for them, and when and how they were to die. But we cannot enter fully into their minds because each generation looks at things in its own way. An American born in 1895 does not see them as does one born in 1945. The older man was brought up in a world uncorrupted by Prohibition, the world of *St. Nicholas Magazine for Boys and Girls;* his early experience with war was limited to the sight of aging Civil War veterans on Memorial Day proudly carrying flags torn by bullets at Bull Run and Gettysburg. It was a horse-drawn world. There were street cars and trains, but a mile was still measured, as it was for the Wife of Bath, by one's own legs or the gait of an ambling horse. However, every generation shares humanity's aspirations and appetites. Bibliographies and microfilm are not needed to recognize the roving eye, the itching palm, Faith, Hope, and Charity.

It is no longer acceptable for an editor to stop at routine identification of persons or casual annotation. His goal is complete understanding, and he hopes to give to his work the final grace of art. Dame Veronica Wedgwood has pointed out: "... truth is not apprehensible nor can it be communicated to another person without the help of art. To pass on any piece of information intelligibly requires a feat in the arrangement of words and ideas."

"From Cicero and Fronto," Harold Laski wrote, "through Mme de Sévigné and Gray and Horace Walpole, Charles Lamb and Byron and Dickens, the great letter-writers have given more pleasure and, perhaps, more insight to their readers than any other type of author save the great novelist and the poet." One can imagine these supreme letter-writers coming upon the stage of critical opinion and receiving salvoes of deserved applause, bowing, retiring, and returning once more. Let us hope that when they return for their tenth encore, a clap or two will be given for the services of those harmless drudges, their editor-accompanists.

Rousseau's Correspondence: Editorial Problems

Ralph A. Leigh

I

It would be idle, in the presence of such a distinguished gathering of editors and potential editors, to dwell unduly on the difficulties inherent in all large-scale scholarly undertakings. As we all know, we have to face a whole series of purely practical problems arising from the sheer dimensions of the enterprise in space and time: for instance, the housing of documents and card-indexes and other stores of information, and with that, the general problem of "information retrieval", as it is now called; or again, the voluminous secondary correspondence, that is to say the complex and intricate negotiations with archivists, librarians, collectors, families, dealers and auctioneers. Along with the problems of bulk, come the problems generated by the time-scale of the operation. Over a period of some thirty years, mere minor matters of formal consistency require an increasing effort; and to descend from something which is clearly not sublime to something which is plainly ridiculous, you discover that the paper of your original notes has frayed and crumbled, that the ink has yellowed and faded, that your early scribble is indecipherable, that your eyes have changed focus or have become blurred and dim. Again, with advancing years, you find you can no longer work fourteen hours a day. The never-ending journeys to remote sources become tiring and tiresome. You can no longer run with the same *élan* after the retreating bus, train or plane: and those enormous folio works of reference, produced in and for a more heroic age, become impossible to lift, or else slip from your enfeebled grasp.

Overlapping in part with these tribulations, there are all the difficulties arising from the dispersal and elusiveness of the material. In addition to the equipment of the scholar, you need the intuitive gifts of the private detective. It is not enough to be a pale reflection of Dom Calmet: you need also to be an apt pupil of Sherlock Holmes.

And then, alas, there is the question of finance. The poor might find it easier to enter the kingdom of heaven, but only the rich can afford to edit an extensive correspondence. The great wealthy foundations, Ford, Rockefeller, Gulbenkian, and the national research councils are reluctant to help a scholar working on his own. They rush to the assistance of institutions, or of impressive-looking teams, which, more often than not, exist only on paper, and whose work tends not infrequently to grind to a halt, while the funds allocated dribble away into overheads and superstructure. These great foundations are suspicious of the scholar working alone, presumably because he offers no guarantees, and they are afraid he will spend their money on riotous living.

My beginnings were difficult and precarious: but in recent years I have had invaluable assistance from UNESCO, the Leverhulme Trust, the British Academy and now the Wolfson

Foundation, who have all paid the salary of a graduate assistant with secretarial skills (not a research assistant: I do the research myself). And for many years my own college (which has so many claims on its resources) has helped me with travelling expenses and in other ways. The Canton of Geneva has also facilitated my work in Switzerland by a much appreciated grant. But even if the foundations do help him, the poor scholar is faced with problems for which the use of foundation funds would be quite improper. Dominated by the quest for hedges of one sort or another against inflation, the modern investor (for you cannot call him a collector) sometimes turns out to be a predatory philistine who denies access. And so, sometimes, the only way to be sure of seeing a manuscript is to buy it. The late Theodore Besterman was wont to complain[1] that he had to spend a considerable part of his private fortune on his edition of Voltaire's correspondence. He was, of course, a collector of both manuscripts and books, as well as an editor: and he was lucky in that he had a private fortune with which to subsidize his work and his collections. Sometimes, even money isn't enough, and you need influence to approach the great or the recalcitrant, and get a glimpse of their papers.

Lastly, one always begins a large-scale work of scholarship too late. It is said, on rather unreliable authority, that a visitor to Cambridge from the United States was so impressed by the emerald, velvety, springy and weedless lawns of one of our colleges, that he sought out the head gardener, and asked him what he should do to obtain a similar result "back home." He was, so it is alleged, somewhat mortified by the answer, which began with the words: "Well, first of all, you start four hundred years ago [. . .]." One has a similar impression when looking over nineteenth-century catalogues, and noting the manuscripts that have disappeared, apparently beyond recall.

So the three golden rules for editing large-scale correspondences are:

1. Be rich, and, if possible, influential too.
2. Be young and vigorous, and make up your mind never to grow old.
3. Always start at least a hundred years before you actually do.

I'm afraid I have broken all these rules, and this accounts in part, not only for the shortcomings of my work, but also for the fact that I am not going to talk about these general difficulties today. Nor am I going to dwell on the fact that, compared with some of the splendidly equipped research factories I have seen or heard of, my edition of Rousseau's correspondence is hardly more than an obsolescent cottage industry.

Instead, I am going to speak about the problems specific to the Rousseau correspondence, which I group under two heads:

1. The difficulties arising from the presence in the field of a bogus monument of scholarship.
2. The special character of the Rousseau manuscripts, and the consequences which that has involved in the establishment of the text.

II

Some forty years ago, when I first became interested in Rousseau, the standard edition of his correspondence was the relatively recent *Correspondance générale de Jean-Jacques Rousseau,* edited from the papers of Théophile Dufour, the Genevan archivist and bibliographer, by his compatriot Pierre-Paul Plan.[2] The first volume appeared in 1924, one year after the death of Dufour, and the twentieth and last volume appeared ten years later, when I was still a first-year under-graduate. It was published in Paris with the aid of a grant from the Institut de France, and was regarded as a monument of scholarship, used and quoted everywhere. Each volume bears on its cover and on its title-page, the statement "collated with the originals," a claim repeated in the footnotes to a large number of individual letters, and explained and developed in Pierre-Paul Plan's preface to his first volume. He points out that the text of Rousseau's correspondence had scarcely changed since Musset-Pathay's edition,[3] which had appeared exactly a century before. The innumerable mistakes, wrong dates, erroneous attributions, the hopelessly corrupt text, with its transpositions, omissions, misreadings all made Rousseau's correspondence quite useless as a tool for scholars. And so, Plan continues, in order to produce a definitive edition, Dufour strove above all else to see the autograph documents themselves, which he transcribed with the genius of the consummate paleographer that he was. In particular, he had thoroughly exploited the riches of the Rousseau archive at Neuchâtel. Of course, he had been unable to discover *all* the original letters; but there were very few which had had to be reproduced from a printed text. When this happened, it was done from the very first printing, in order to reduce error to the minimum. However, the number of Rousseau's letters which Dufour knew only through a printed text, Plan emphasized, was only a small proportion of the whole. And so, he concluded, his edition had two important basic characteristics: for the first time, the whole of Rousseau's correspondence was brought together, as far as it was then possible; and for the first time, it provided an authentic text on which scholars could rely.

Well-nigh impeccable principles, leading to a consummation devoutly to be wished. Unfortunately, as I have shown else-where,[4] almost every one of these statements is false. Indeed, it is difficult, though no doubt not impossible, to believe that

Plan did not know them to be false, since he was actually preparing the material himself, and was fully aware of all those cases in which he was sending to the press barely edited paste-ups of previously printed texts. How many of the defects of this edition are due to Dufour himself, how many to the fact that Dufour's materials were not in a fit state for publication, how many to the over-eagerness of his family to erect a monument to his memory, how many to the sheer incompetence and negligence of Pierre-Paul Plan, it would be difficult and no doubt invidious to establish. What is clear is that, apart from a relatively small number of letters accurately transcribed by Dufour personally from the originals, the great majority of the texts were not printed from Rousseau's manuscripts nor even from the first printing (I pass by the naïve assumption that the first printing necessarily offers the best text of a letter, to concentrate on the element of truth in that badly-phrased assumption, i.e. that a reproduction of the first printing is likely to be less accurate than the first printing itself).

I won't go into detail here: but imagine our surprise when we discover that a large number of Dufour-Plan's texts are reprinted (with additional errors) from that very edition of Musset-Pathay's which Plan had reproached his predecessors for using, and which he had denounced as inadequate. Our surprise is raised to the second degree when we discover that Musset-Pathay's texts, with few exceptions, are mostly reprinted from the Geneva edition of 1782 and its supplements,[5] from the various collections published by Du Peyrou from 1790 onwards,[6] and from other works. Why didn't Dufour-Plan at least use these instead of Musset-Pathay?

With regard to the letters received by Rousseau, the situation is even worse. A great-grandson of Paul Moultou (Rousseau's friend and co-executor), Georges Streckeisen-Moultou, had published in 1861 two volumes of letters received by Rousseau,[7] selected from the extensive collection at Neuchâtel. To be absolutely fair to him, Streckeisen was the worst kind of nineteenth-century editor. He censors the letters of his great-grandfather when they express unorthodox opinions, he rewrites in his own style passages which offend his taste or sense of grammatical correctness, omits other passages which he cannot understand or cannot decipher (all without any hint or indication to the reader), confidently misreads other passages, confidently ascribes wrong dates to undated or partly undated letters, and even on occasion to those which are quite clearly dated. Dufour knew all this: from time to time he collated a text published by Streckeisen with the original at Neuchâtel, and expressed his condemnation of the editing of his predecessor in no uncertain terms. This did not prevent him or Plan in most cases from reproducing Streckeisen's text. In some instances, he adds "collated with the original." This statement, alas, is also usually false. All that has been done for most letters is to verify the date and the signature. Indeed, not infrequently, the Dufour-Plan text is actually worse than Streckeisen's, for additional errors have crept in: and they have compounded their felony by actually omitting some of the texts included by Streckeisen. The strange thing is, all the texts used by Streckeisen were and are still at Neuchâtel, whose treasures, as Plan assures us, were all fully exploited by Dufour. If so, why were Streckeisen's texts used instead of the originals? And if it were not so, why say so? Not is it true that the edition was as complete as possible. A very large number of available letters, mainly received by Rousseau, but also some written by him, were omitted.

Even worse, in some ways, was the treatment of Rousseau's own letters. But this question is inextricably linked with my second point, the special character of the Rousseau manuscripts, which I will deal with later. At the moment, I simply want to say that the Dufour-Plan edition of Rousseau's correspondence was, in the upshot, one of the most extraordinary hoaxes ever perpetrated on the world of learning. My early pre-war work on Rousseau had shown me some of its shortcomings, but I was very far from realizing its true character. At first, I thought it might be possible simply to issue a volume of corrigenda. Gradually, as the truth began to dawn on me, I realized that this was out of the question, and that the whole correspondence would have to be done again from scratch. But the existence of a respected monument edited by two Genevan worthies was a serious obstacle. Some sections of Genevan opinion did not take at all kindly to the exposure of two local heroes of scholarship, both remembered with affection and respect in their native city; whilst there was considerable prejudice in some quarters against a mere foreigner (and not a *francophone* at that) presuming to edit the correspondence of Geneva's greatest writer. It was said that a foreigner could not possibly do the job as well as a Genevan, that in any case Dufour-Plan was not as bad as had been implied, and that a new edition was an unnecessary waste of effort. It was partly for these reasons, and also because there was a historical interest attached to the form in which Rousseau's correspondence had been known and used, that I decided to point out in my critical notes the errors of the last standard text of each letter (generally Dufour-Plan's). I could have said, of course, that in so doing I was only following the example of Dufour himself, who pointed out with great relish the errors of preceding editors, even in many cases where they were not errors at all - and thereby hangs a tale to which I will return in a moment or two. The late Theodore Besterman, who was largely unaware of the special circumstances, and was certainly ignorant of the full extent of Dufour-Plan's editorial malpractices, disapproved my doing so: and certainly not all editors of correspondences will feel obliged to point out previous errors as a matter of course. Besterman was quite right in disliking the habit of showing up one's predecessors simply for the sake of doing so, in a spirit of self-satisfaction or self-congratulation. We are all human, and all liable to make mistakes. But the shortcomings of Dufour-Plan were not just a few slips scattered through a large body of accurate texts. They are almost omnipresent, and arise from a culpable neglect of the very editorial principles which they professed. Moreover, unlike Besterman, I was dealing with a recent so-called scholarly edition, not a superannuated antique like Moland, Beuchot or Kehl.

III

I come now to my second point, the special character of the manuscripts of Rousseau's letters. I take as my cue the well-known passage in the *Confessions* in which he explains how difficult he found the art of writing:

> It is only with the most unbelievable difficulty that my ideas fall into place in my head. [. . .] That is why I find writing so extremely difficult. My manuscripts, full of corrections, scribbled, tangled, indecipherable, bear witness to the effort they have cost me. Not one that I have not had to transcribe four or five times before sending it to the printer. [. . .] That again is why I am better in works which require preparation than in those which need a certain lightness of touch, like letters, a form which I have never been able to hit off well - having to write them really tortures me. I can't write a single letter on the most trivial subject without tiring myself out for hours on end [. . .] [8]

Anyone who has had more than superficial acquaintance with Rousseau's manuscripts knows that this statement in the *Confessions* is literally true. Rousseau, as I have so often said, is the Flaubert of the eighteenth century. His drafts are a formidable mass of deletions, marginal and interlinear insertions, cancellations, second, third and fourth thoughts, re-drafting and rearrangement. Confining ourselves to the letters, we must note that other factors were at work besides the urge for literary perfection or for the perfect and perfectly accurate formulation of thought. When Rousseau became a celebrity, the most conspicuous ingredients of his fame were his love of paradox and the warmth of his style: "l'écrivain le plus éloquent de son siècle," - even his enemies (except Voltaire) admitted he was that. The consequence was that everyone expected his lightest utterance to carry the hall-mark of this "éloquence," and this certainly increased his inhibitions about composing even the most trivial letters. Later, the symptoms of his neuroses also began to affect his drafts, chiefly in the form of nervous indecision, which entailed the repeated insertion, deletion and reinstatement of the same word, sometimes three or four times in succession.

What bearing does this have on the editor's task? Theoretically, a Rousseau letter passed through at least four states or stages:

1. a *premier jet* - preliminary jottings, often disconnected. Comparatively few of these have survived.

2. one or more *brouillons* - heavily corrected roughs, the basic text, and often the successive alterations, being written generally in barely decipherable scribble.

3. a *mise au net* - a fair copy, in a semi-calligraphied hand, kept as a record, or for other reasons.

4. the missive letter *(original autographe)* - the document actually sent to the addressee, bearing generally an address page or leaf with seal and (if sent through the post) various postal endorsements.

Of course, not all these states have been preserved for all the letters. Nor are they exhaustive or even hard and fast. For instance, a manuscript which begins as a fair copy may degenerate into a rough. Again, what was originally intended to be the missive letter, complete with address, may have been revised by Rousseau as he read it over. One of the forms of courtesy favoured by this prickly and meticulous mind was never to send a letter which carried more than one or two minor corrections. The missive letters are not all absolutely immaculate: but most of them are nearly so. Those that did not satisfy this criterion were copied out again, the substandard original being retained. Such a "failed missive" I call a *premier état corrigé* (corrected first state).

This, however, is not the end of the matter. When Rousseau made up his mind to write his *Confessions,* he decided to compile a letter-book *(copie-de-lettres)* as supporting evidence *(pièces justificatives)* for his statements. And so, during his exile at Môtiers, throughout the long, snow-bound winters (perhaps, though not certainly, as early as 1762-63), he began copying out the letters he had written and received. But, of course, as far as his own letters were concerned, he no longer had before him the text actually sent. All he had were the various early jottings, drafts, fair copies and corrected first states which he had kept. Those, of course, were by no means identical with the letters actually sent. Nor did Rousseau in fact make exact copies even of the materials he had before him. Sometimes, reading over his roughs and fair copies, he remembered the changes he had made, or (more probably) arrived at a text close to that of the missive letter by solving the stylistic problems of his drafts in the same way as he had done before. But in other cases, he solved the problems differently, and in addition he sometimes allowed himself the luxury of a few supplementary alterations, generally (but not always) purely formal. Moreover, such features of the missive letter as an extra paragraph or a last-minute post-script had usually not been recorded on the draft or fair copy, and so could not find their way into the letter-book. For all these reasons, the letter-book texts are different in many cases both from the drafts and the missives. Rousseau's correspondence must be one of the few cases in which the letters (at least for the period 1755-62) lead posthumous lives, as it were, and in which the text continues to evolve after the letters have been despatched. The same consideration applies to a small number of important letters which Rousseau intended to include in his complete works. In these instances, he kept a fair copy which he touched up from time to time. This is the case, for example, with the famous letter on optimism which he sent to Voltaire on 18 August 1756.[9]

Rousseau's treatment in his letter-book of the letters received by him leads to similar results. Here, of course, he had the missive letters before him, but here again his copies were not literal. First of all, he normalized spelling and punctuation in accordance with his own fairly consistent practice. Secondly, he corrected the syntax and improved the style of the originals. In the interests of clarity or euphony, he did not hesitate to transpose words or phrases, to sub-stitute more appropriate terms, to alter tenses, to rectify or introduce concords where they were false or had been omitted. Finally, he found the hand-writing of some of his correspondents difficult to decipher, and misread certain words, or guessed wrongly. And in the case of both series of letters, to the deliberate changes he made we must add the usual errors of the copyist from which Jean-Jacques was not altogether exempt: omissions, slips of the pen, and so on.

Before proceeding, I should like to draw attention to two characteristics of the letter-book which were to have, in different ways, undesirable repercussions of the history of the letters. First of all, many of Rousseau's correspondents did not date their letters, or dated them only by the day of week. Rousseau sometimes had great difficulty in arranging them, as he tried to do, in chronological order, and he was sometimes wrong. This has had an effect not only on the history of the correspondence, but in some cases also on the composition of Part II of the *Confessions.*

Secondly, the letter-book copies are in Rousseau's best writing and easy to read, easier in many cases than the originals. This seemingly innocent fact was also to have unfortunate consequences, as indeed was the case with the multiplicity of manuscript sources itself.

To understand what happened, we must go back as far as the Geneva edition of 1782, its supplements, and the various collections of letters published by Du Peyrou from 1790 onwards.

It was, of course, Pierre-Alexandre Du Peyrou who was the principal architect of Rousseau's correspondence, not Musset-Pathay or Dufour. Without the devoted efforts of this gouty, deaf, free-thinking and above all devoted literary executor of Jean-Jacques, the correspondence of Rousseau, as it was known for a hundred and fifty years, indeed, in many ways, as we have it today, would have been inconceivable. I am not referring simply to his services as a custodian of Rousseau's papers, invaluable as those services were. He did much more. As soon as Rousseau died, Du Peyrou began to collect the originals of his letters from as many addressees as possible, and, where they declined to part with the originals, badgered them or their heirs for copies. In addition, as the years went by, he enriched his editions with clean transcripts made by him or his secretaries from the rough drafts or fair copies now in his possession - no mean task in the cases of the drafts, though naturally he did not bother with the variants, recording only the final readings. Unfortunately, Du Peyrou never specifies the nature of his sources, so that it is impossible to tell whether we are reading the text of the missive letter, the text of a copy of the missive, the text of a rough draft, the text of a fair copy, or the text of a letter known only through an early printed source.

This defect was compounded to the nth degree by Dufour-Plan, who used Du Peyrou (as transmitted by Musset-Pathay), Streckeisen-Moultou and a large number of secondary printings or nineteenth-century manuscript copies, most of them in nineteenth-century spelling. I regret to say that sometimes Dufour-Plan give a spurious air of authenticity to their texts by substituting for the nineteenth-century forms of their sources the *ancien régime* verb-endings, "-oit," "-oient," and the noun and adjectival endings "-ns." Similarly, "-ms" replaces "-mps" in words like "tems." This spurious aging is not always consistent, even within the confines of a single letter. I should perhaps add at this point that in order to avoid what Eugène Ritter, another Genevan scholar, called the "cacagraphie" of eighteenth-century manuscripts, Dufour once suggested homogenizing them by adopting the spelling of the contemporary Academy dictionary. He meant presumably the edition of 1762. To be absolutely logical, letters written before that date should have been *gleichgeschaltet* in accordance with the preceding edition (1740), which would have given them a decidedly archaic look compared with the others. But I don't think Dufour intended this. He was suggesting that the letters should all be dressed in the uniform of 1762. The least said about this proposal (which was not actually adopted), the better. But as far as spurious aging is concerned, it was certainly carried out, sporadically, in his edition.

Finally, I should add that, because of its superior legibility, Dufour-Plan often preferred the text of the letter-book copies to the originals, though the latter were all available.

The text of the Dufour-Plan edition is then, not only inaccurate, it is also extremely heterogeneous and arbitrary in its presentation. A further turn of the screw was given when, as happened from time to time, a missive letter turned up which had previously been known to Dufour only through

Musset-Pathay. Where the Musset-Pathay texts were derived
from Du Peyrou's transcriptions of Rousseau's drafts, there
were naturally differences, sometimes quite considerable
ones, between the two texts. Dufour thereupon solemnly
took it upon himself to record, in a censorious frame of mind,
the "mistakes" made by previous editors. But in most cases
they weren't mistakes at all, as a little thought would have
shown, but genuine author's variants derived from an earlier
state of the letter - in a word, variants which should have been
incorporated into the critical apparatus.

IV

The principal textual features of my edition emerge by
implication and antithesis from this discussion. For each
letter, I have tried to collect and evaluate the known manuscripts. I have taken as my basic text that of the letter actually
sent to the addressee (sometimes known through the document itself, sometimes through an authentic copy). I have
then given in my critical notes the variants from the other
states of the letter (unless one or more of these states is so
different as to require separate printing). I have also sometimes given variants from contemporary copies where these
seem important. In the eighteenth century, letters sometimes
circulated widely in manuscript before being printed, and it is
often useful to ascertain the form in which Rousseau's letters
became known to the public, particularly in view of his
complaints that they were falsified, which they sometimes
were. As a corollary, I have tried to discover when a letter
was first printed, and to give variants from important printings
where this seemed appropriate. In the list of sources, the
basic text reproduced is indicated by an asterisk; sources
which I have not seen, but which are known to exist, or to
have existed, are enclosed within square brackets.
This aspect of my edition, the identification of the states

of the various texts and the presentation of such a large body of variants, is perhaps its most novel feature. It is certainly the most laborious. But there are rewards and compensations. One is the fascination of immediacy, of seeing for instance Jean-Jacques cooling from the white heat of fury in his drafts to the glacial sarcasm of his final version: or to visualize him striding about the moors of Derbyshire, jotting down a few lines for the exordium of his famous letter to Hume[10] on the fly-leaf or end-paper of a book on botany he happened to be carrying. Or again to watch the ripples caused by a detected and eradicated verbal repetition spreading ever wider through the text of an entire paragraph. Not infrequently there are results of a different order: an important passage cancelled for various reasons, (in the instance I am going to quote, undoubtedly out of prudence). In a famous letter to the Marquis de Mirabeau,[11] he informs his correspondent that his economic system would have unexpected results if implemented, would lead us to "des pays bien différens de ceux où vous prétendez aller." This enigmatic remark was amplified in a cancelled passage, hitherto unknown: "Aussi je suis fâché de vous dire que tant que la monarchie subsistera en France il n'y sera jamais adopté" - an unexpected parallel to a well-known passage and footnote in *Emile,* prophesying the impending downfall of the great monarchies of Europe.[12]

V

I ought now perhaps to say a word or two about the editorial principles which I have adopted. Everyone knows that it is impossible to print an eighteenth-century manuscript as it stands, and the problem of presentation becomes acute when one is dealing not with a single author but with hundreds of different writers all with their own mannerisms. There is also the secondary problem of letters known only through nineteenth-century copies or printed texts, the characteristics of which are those of a nineteenth-century copyist, editor or printer.

An easy way out would be complete modernization. To this I am resolutely opposed. An eighteenth-century correspondence such as Rousseau's, including thousands of letters from people in every walk of life, is an invaluable treasure-house of linguistic raw material which must be scrupulously preserved for the use of historians of the language, historical phoneticians, morphologists, lexicographers, syntacticians, and the like. I could give many examples. I shall quote just one. Modern Frenchmen, when they use the expression "sang-froid," think in terms of "cool blood," but an eighteenth-century Frenchman, quite frequently, thought he was talking of "cool sense." Modernization also obscures eighteenth-century habits about concords, especially mute ones, the treatment of the past participle, and the confusion between tenses which offer convergent forms. Indeed, a modernizing editor would often be forced to choose where the original clearly left matters open or doubtful. Modernization would also destroy valuable evidence about pre-Revolutionary pronunciation, including liaison.

A certain amount of *toilette,* however, which helps the reader without distorting the linguistic material, is permissible. I have in general adopted the modern distinction between *i* and *j,* *u* and *v,* not only for the reader's convenience but because in many hands the distinction is indeterminate, and you cannot tell which was intended. With "s," the problem is rather different. There are at least three or four types of "s" used in eighteenth-century manuscripts, not to speak of the older double "ss" which survived, like the intervocalic or initial long-tailed "s," into the nineteenth century. I have not preserved the long-tailed "s" or the old double "ss," but have had trouble with capitals. When Rousseau was particularly ceremonious or particularly irritated (and the two often go together, since anger often drove him to frigid formality), his missive letters were copied out with particular care, and have a much higher density of random capital "S's." I decided that this was a psychological peculiarity worth preserving, but it entailed respecting random capitalization throughout the correspondence, something particularly tricky in the case of "s" and "c" where the difference is frequently simply one of size. With some correspondents, there are peculiar difficulties. Mme de Verdelin, for instance, perhaps on account of her signature, always writes a capital "V" wherever the letter occurs, even in the middle of a word. I have not humoured her in this respect. Again, for all correspondents, I start sentences with capitals, and bestow capitals on proper names.

As a general rule, I have preserved the punctuation and accentuation of the originals, even where it is neither consistent nor rational. One or two points are perhaps just worth noting, since I have not seen them commented on elsewhere. Some correspondents, and even Jean-Jacques himself, seem to have used the edge of the paper as a punctuation mark, instead of a light stop such as a comma. Since the edge of my paper does not coincide with theirs, I have sometimes felt it necessary to supply commas where absolutely necessary or highly desirable. Again, there is one feature of eighteenth-century manuscript punctuation, the loss of which I greatly regret: the question mark or the exclamation mark mounted, not over a full-stop, as in modern usage, but over a comma or even occasionally over a semi-colon. I should have liked to reproduce this elegant and logical refinement: but it proved to be technically difficult. On the rare occasions where the writer's punctuation was really too irrational to preserve, I have modified it. For instance, the abbé Cahagne puts a full stop regularly after every three words and never at the end of a sentence. I have called him to order. Mme de Verdelin hardly punctuates at all, and hardly ever lets air or daylight into her prose. On the rare occasions when she does so, she often puts a great thick comma or semi-colon at the end of a paragraph. Here and there, smaller commas appear sporadically in her text. I have taken it upon myself to ventilate her letters a little, to lend her a few commas, and much more rarely a full stop or two. I have done so sparingly, for it seemed right to preserve the headlong or breathless character of her utterances, whilst giving the reader a little assistance.

As for accents, eighteenth-century correspondents use them less frequently, and according to personal systems which differ both from eighteenth-century printed usage and from the rules fastened on the language in the nineteenth-century. I have not supplied or changed accentuation, except in final syllables of words of two syllables or more, where the pronunciation cannot be doubted. For instance, I always print "j'ai donne" as "j'ai donné."

All this applies, of course, only to eighteenth-century manuscripts or printed sources. Unlike the late Theodore Besterman, I think it interesting (for the reasons given) to preserve the characteristics even of an eighteenth-century copyist or printer. I agree with him, however, in modernizing nineteenth-century copies or printings. Unlike Dufour-Plan, I have not indulged in spurious aging of such texts, though of course it would have been quite easy to do so. And so modernization in my edition immediately warns the reader that the text he is reading is that of a late copy.

VI

I ought finally to say a word or two about the annotation. The late Theodore Besterman was against extensive annotation, and it must be admitted that compared with mine his is a plain text. Of course, I don't give simple biographical notes on people like Sophocles, Virgil, Homer, Dante, Petrarch, Tasso, Montaigne and Racine, though it is necessary in some contexts to identify them. However, one of the problems of

Rousseau's correspondence is the large number of individuals who have left no footprints in the sands of time, let alone in standard works of reference.

The bulk of the information provided in my notes comes from eighteenth-century sources: dictionaries and grammars, gazettes, almanacs, journals, legal *factums,* placets and petitions, manuscript registers of births, marriages and deaths, manuscript correspondences, the manuscript minute books of councils and other bodies in Geneva, Lausanne, Neuchâtel, Berne, Paris, Strasbourg, Lyons and other French provincial towns such as Chartres and Dijon, and so on. Where later sources are used, they include specialized monographs and genealogies often printed in strictly limited editions. The bibliographical information comes principally from the books themselves, most of which I have seen and handled. I have worked on the assumption that most users of the correspondence will not have ready access to most of this source material, and indeed that many of them will not have access to any of it at all. Of course, I don't need to warn an audience like this of the dangers of relying on so-called standard works of reference. Most of us know how they are compiled, and how unreliable they can be. To take one simple example: Tissot was a well-known eighteenth-century doctor with a European reputation, and you would think that the reference books would at least get his Christian names right. Most of them list him as "Simon-André," but the register of his birth shows that he was baptised "Samuel-Auguste-André-David." Again, my amateur lexicographical researches revealed to me a curious fact, no doubt well known to specialists in the field, but not, I find, to French scholars generally, and that is the surprising number of definitions in the Academy Dictionary of 1762 which have been silently adopted and reproduced word for word by Littré.

What should be included in an edition of an eighteenth-century correspondence? Another speaker will be addressing you on the question of when is a letter not a letter. There is, of course, a *prima facie* problem. My principle is to include any text which was actually sent to the addressee: that means including open letters and *lettres ostensibles* when they were actually sent. Take, for instance, the letter to Marc Chappuis of 26 May 1763,[13] referred to by Rousseau's opponents as "le tocsin de la sédition." The letter was clearly intended for the general public: so much so that, although Chappuis refused to divulge its contents or to show it to anybody, Rousseau made sure it would be known by providing copies for circulation in Geneva: but it was actually sent to Chappuis and so must be included. I have also included letters which were intended to be sent, though not finally despatched for one reason or another. I have not generally included dedicatory letters, but I have reproduced hand-written messages in presentation copies of books where these fulfilled the same function as a *billet d'envoi.* I have also included important letters about Rousseau exchanged between third parties.

Finally, I have printed the letters in a single chronological sequence. I know the arguments for doing otherwise. Dufour-Plan introduced the novel principle (inconsistently applied) of following each letter by its answer, regardless of date. The idea may seem to some extent rational, but its application leads to chaos where a correspondence consists of a continuous tissue, and where, owing partly to varying distances and the vagaries of the post, there is so much leap-frogging between letters and their answers. On the other hand, Mr. Lewis, whom we are so delighted to have with us today, has ably defended the principle of arranging Walpole's exchanges by addressees, partly on the grounds that Walpole wrote in a significantly different manner to his various friends, partly because certain exchanges present a unity which it is undesirable to destroy. Similar arguments might be applied to Jean-Jacques. At least, it is clear he wrote in a different vein to Mme d'Houdetot, to Mme de Boufflers, to the Luxembourgs, to Moultou, to Du Peyrou and to Marc-Michel Rey, and that these exhanges exhibit a certain unity. And no doubt the letters would have been easier to present in this way since that is basically how they tend to be preserved in Neuchâtel and Geneva and other places. However, in the case of Rousseau, there seemed to be a greater advantage in bringing out what was in his mind at any given moment: hence my preference for a strictly chronological treatment, which also (but only incidentally) has the advantage of avoiding unassimilated residues.

In a word, what I have tried to supply in my edition is a sincere text, with virtually complete textual variants, the elements of a history of the letters and their publication, together with a comprehensive annotation, biographical, bibliographical, linguistic, explaining references to contemporary events and tracing literary allusions and quotations. One bewildered though favourable reviewer once asked "Who will need all this information?" The answer, of course, is nobody, in the sense of no single person. But I have not edited the letters for a single person. And I hope that a great many users of the work will find some of the information provided helpful.

I'm not saying that every editor of an eighteenth-century correspondence should take the same trouble: in any case, he won't have the same problems. But this is Jean-Jacques Rousseau, the prophet and the critic of modern times: not only an influential thinker of outstanding importance, whose work occupies a strategic position in the history of western civilization, but a great writer and a fascinating personality; and so he and his correspondence are a triple source of enduring interest and perennial controversy. It is for these reasons that, although this morning Mr. Bell has been tolling the death knell of large-scale undertakings such as mine, I have sought to place in the hands of scholars a research tool on which, I hope, they can rely.

NOTES

1 For this and other references to Besterman's views, see his paper in *Les Editions de Correspondances, colloque du 20 avril 1968*, Paris, Colin, pp. 8-18.

2 *Correspondance générale de J.-J. Rousseau, Collationnée sur les originaux, annotée et commentée par Théophile Dufour* [et par Pierre-Paul Plan], Paris, Armand Colin, 20 vols., 1924-34.

3 *Oeuvres complètes de J.-J. Rousseau, mises dans un nouvel ordre, avec des notes historiques et des éclaircissements; par V.D. Musset-Pathay*, Paris, chez P. Dupont, 22 vols., 1823-24. The *Correspondance* occupies vols. 18-22. More correspondence was included in vol. I of the two volumes of *Oeuvres inédites*, Paris, P. Dupont, 1825.

4 R.A. Leigh, "Vers une nouvelle edition de la correspondance de Jean-Jacques Rousseau," *Annales de la Société Jean-Jacques Rousseau*, 35 (1959-62), 263-80.

5 *Collection complète des Oeuvres de J.-J. Rousseau* [...], Geneva, 1782, published simultaneously in three formats, 4o, 8o and 12o. Some volumes are dated 1780. Supplements appeared in 1782 and 1789.

6 Du Peyrou added appreciably to the corpus of the correspondence in his editions of the works published at Neuchâtel by L. Fauche-Borel. The bibliography of these editions has not yet been completely elucidated.

7 G. Streckeisen-Moultou, *J.-J. Rousseau, ses amis et ses ennemis*, Paris, Calmann-Levy, [1865], 2 vols.

8 *Confessions* III, (éd. Bernard Gagnebin et Marcel Raymond), Paris, Bibliothèque de la Pléiade, Gallimard, 1962, p. 114.

9 *Correspondance complète de J.-J. Rousseau*, ed. R.A. Leigh, IV, No. 424, 37-71.

10 *Ibid.*, XXX, No. 5274, 29-54, and No. 5274 ter, 81-82.

11 *Ibid.*, XXXIII, No. 5991 and 5991 bis, note critique, 56, 241 and 246.

12 *Emile* III, Paris, Bibliothèque de la Pléiade, Gallimard, 1968, IV, p. 468.

13 *Correspondance complète*, XVI, No. 2726, 245-50.

The Letters of
Sir Walter Scott:
Problems and Opportunities

Alan Bell

Mr. Lewis's admirable introduction to our proceedings, which will show many all-too-obvious contrasts with my own in age, experience and wisdom, was concerned with a long, long task which is now nearing a triumphant conclusion. The greater part of my paper will deal with an editorial problem which has not yet achieved the dignity of becoming a project, and perhaps may eventually be reckoned impracticable. That is, I hope, no reason why some of the problems - which are generally applicable - should not be discussed in advance of a decision that ought not to be taken for several years to come.

It was originally suggested that I might speak of my work on the letters of Sydney Smith. This task, which is still continuing, has occupied much of my leisure for nearly ten years. It will eventually result in a four-volume edition of his letters, doubling the number of texts previously collected and substantially revising the two volumes of my predecessor, Nowell C. Smith.[1] It will in 1979 also produce a biography for which I naughtily, and in reverse of the usual editorial practice, diverted myself from purely epistolary studies. I have, however, recently written about the textual history, current progress and literary justification of my work on these two thousand or more letters, in the *Bulletin of the John Rylands Library* for Autumn 1976. There seemed at present to be little more to say about the private work which has given me so much pleasure and amusement.

Knowing, however, that my fellow-speakers would be concerning themselves with work on much larger correspondences, I thought I would instead attempt a perhaps premature report on some work I have been doing as an Assistant Keeper of the National Library of Scotland, towards compiling a Survey of the Letters of Sir Walter Scott. I do so with the permission of the Librarian, but - as you will realize - much of what I have to say is only my personal opinion of the problems and opportunities which present themselves. This is no mere official disclaimer, as I am always acutely aware that I am not a Scott scholar in any conventional sense of the term, finding myself lacking a widely-based critical understanding of his writings and without the full literary knowledge which would guarantee a better assessment of his letters than I can achieve. My approach - and I hope it may be thought a distinctive and useful one - is that of an archivist who enjoys the privilege of looking after the great collections of Sir Walter Scott's correspondence and literary manuscripts in Edinburgh, and who is aware of the duty of making these holdings known as efficiently and usefully as possible to the world of scholarship.

At the time of the 1971 celebrations of the bicentenary of Scott's birth, there was a growing feeling that something ought to be done about the Centenary Edition of *Letters of Sir Walter Scott* published by Constable between 1932 and

1937 under the senior editorship of Sir Herbert Grierson. The question was put by Dr. D.S. Hewitt of the University of Aberdeen in a paper to the Scott Bicentenary Conference.[2] Since then Dr. Hewitt and I have been working, with the backing of the National Library of Scotland and the goodwill of many friendly scholars, to find an answer.

The twelve volumes of the Centenary Edition, containing the texts of some 4,800 of Scott's letters, generously disposed on the page and supplied with footnotes, lists and other apparatus, look an impressive shelf-full: a mine of information about Scott, his work, his circle and his period. But the reality is very different. There are a number of objections to it. It has long been out of print and it is often not readily accessible to younger scholars.[3] There is no index. The detailed presentation of the letters in respect of transcription, annotation, dating and editorial consistency leaves much to be desired. The chronological sequence of the entire correspondence cannot be adequately worked out, as there are several sub-groups of letters inserted at the ends of inappropriate volumes. Above all it is incomplete, and incomplete on a really massive scale.

Nothing survives in Edinburgh of the administrative correspondence of the edition, but it is possible that the publishers' archives may eventually help to fill out the story. They may show what happened, in publishing terms, to a financially under-endowed project when the bulk of letters discovered during the period of publication far outran the limit of twelve volumes which Constable's had prudently set. The need to have a substantial group of volumes ready for the centenary year of Scott's death, 1932, obviously prevented the thorough planning which (even in the days before epistolary scholarship had been elevated to a more systematic level) should surely have been recognized as desirable. It would be wrong to labour these points now (few things are more time-consuming than editors lovingly but wearisomely detailing their predecessors' shortcomings). One must admit that with all its faults the Centenary Edition represented a substantial advance, however inadequate, in Scott studies; much valuable work in the last forty years has been based on it. But its strategic blunders are so large and obvious that other editors have much to learn from them. My own opinion is that the Centenary Edition is jerry-built, ill-planned and ill-executed, and in many ways a slum.

It is some comfort that one of its defects will be remedied before long, as an index is to be published. This obvious lack has long been remarked on. During the war the National Library commissioned one from W.M. Parker, Grierson's chief assistant as editor and a knowledgeable student of Scott; this proved to be unsatisfactory and remains on hand-written slips. However, Dr. J.C. Corson, a scholar of quite different calibre who occupies a special place in Scott studies both on his own account and as honorary librarian of Abbots-ford, has completed a very full index to the twelve-volume printed text, which is imminently expected from the Oxford University Press. Just as Sir Herbert Grierson, when he had shaken off his editorial toils, wrote a life of Scott "supple-mentary to and corrective of" Lockhart's biography.[4] Dr. Corson's index will, I gather, contain notes supplementary to and corrective of the Centenary Edition: they are sorely needed. The compiler has kindly informed me that his 8,000 notes will occupy about 400 double-column pages; and the index, which will be about the same length, is so full as to form an epitome of the twelve volumes. It contains many identifications of obscure persons, with entries in chrono-logical order correcting the faulty sequences of the original presentation.

Dr. Corson's index will at last complete a publication which commenced in 1932, and will help to correct many of the errors of commission. The errors of omission are still more serious. Underestimating the material available and restricted by the limitation to twelve volumes, the Centenary editors had to be increasingly selective. Only a tenth of Volume XII, dated on the spine "1831-1832," contains letters of those years; the remaining 400 pages fill gaps in the earlier coverage. The editors therefore rejected a good deal of useful material, some of it of great importance. Fortunately their transcriptions, mainly in typescript and all very crudely set out, were given to the National Library; these make up four volumes, usually known to Scott scholars as the "Grierson rejects," which run to some 1,500 quarto pages in all. The National Library holds many other texts acquired since the time of the edition, and has systematically pursued Scott material offered for sale. Many other libraries have acquired new letters; the massive holdings of family papers in the Scottish Record Office are a very fruitful source; several substantial private collections have been built up, and single letters and small groups of correspondence are coming to light the world over.

The possibilities are almost limitless. Scott became famous early in life and his letters soon had a celebrity appeal. He was an efficient and prolific correspondent with official business as well as literary and personal affairs to swell the bulk of his letter-writing. His incoming correspondence survives intact in the National Library, with thousands of letters (which would present special editorial problems) indicating incidentally the range of outgoing items as yet unaccounted for. In 1971 Dr. Hewitt estimated that there were some three thousand additional unpublished or uncollected letters. That is almost certainly an underestimate. We might perhaps say that between four and five thousand letters may be found to add to the 4,800 of the Centenary Edition; the total may be even more. The incoming letters have to be taken into account, and (although it is impossible - and unwise - to be specific) we may end up with something between twelve and fifteen thousand units of information: round figures which at least give an idea of the massive but (especially to an audience such as this) not unprecedented scale of the problem. We are faced with exercise in documentation on a very large scale indeed.

What then could be done? It was clear that it would be a useful and interesting task to make a systematic attempt to record all the supplementary information. It was almost as clear that, because of its preeminent holdings of manuscript correspondence and its responsibility towards a figure so important in the national literary heritage, the National Library of Scotland with its administrative as well as bibliographical resources would be the best place in which to devise, house and maintain such a record. With the encouragement of the Librarian and the blessing of a committee of representative literary scholars, the Survey of the Letters of Sir Walter Scott was duly inaugurated. It would be misleading to think of the survey as a "factory," as most of the work is done by a single investigator (myself) with the invaluable occasional help of a specialist scholar (Dr. Hewitt) to encourage and advise. This limitation of manpower is matched by a limitation of aim. The Survey is conceived of very much as a Survey and not as an Edition - the Survey is not an Edition, whether supplementary, corrective or completely revised. An edition is only one of the opportunities I would like to speak about later; at present the Survey presents us with sufficient work and problems to keep us busily occupied. Whether any further work on the letters arises from it or not, the Survey itself will be of obvious value to scholars who must in any case visit the Library and particularly the Department of Manuscripts when undertaking any serious work on Scott. And it is an incidental benefit that this useful registration of information will help to answer some of the most important questions which must be faced by any potential editor who is anxious to avoid the mistake of inadequate planning which is at the root of the Centenary Edition's faults. At present the

Survey takes the form of a series of 8" x 5" index cards which
record the direction (to or from), correspondent, Centenary
reference (if any), manuscript location and reference, and the
date (and for Scott's outgoing letters, the place of writing).
This can be accommodated on a single headline, with some
standardizations of information, and debates of identification
of people and dates kept to a minimum. Lower down the
card are given the first line or phrase of the letter, details of
postmarks, watermarks, and other relevant physical details.
The card system can be expanded or rearranged as necessary.
The layout has been devised with some sort of interim
publication in list form in mind, but the details have still to
be decided on. One of my colleagues in the Library, Mr. Ian
Cunningham, is joint editor of the forthcoming *David Livingstone: A Catalogue of Documents*, a bulky checklist prepared
by the David Livingstone Documentation Project with the
backing of several research funds; the Livingstone Project's
techniques and eventual publications will help us to see how
best to proceed.

So far we have some seven thousand cards on file, and we
are still concentrating on the holdings of the National Library
itself, recording correspondence both ways; most of it has
been catalogued, and indexed in groups by correspondent,
but not individually, letter by letter. When the National
Library's holdings have been fully incorporated we should
have a very firm base from which we can gradually spread
out enquiries over a world-wide field of libraries, archives,
institutional and private collections. Approaching such an
exercise from the point of view of international library co-
operation, we should, I hope, be able to advise colleagues and
friends about the dates, addressees and subjects of letters
which have been wrongly or inadequately catalogued, for
Scott's handwriting and his presentation of his letters often
give rise to error. Such advice as we have so far been able to
provide, grounded on counterpart letters in the National

Library of Scotland, seems to have been much appreciated by custodians. This mutually beneficial exchange of information will do much to secure for the Survey the photocopies which are essential for indexing purposes when personal inspection of the documents is impossible. There may of course be a number of objections from other institutions to making copies of their letters generally available in the National Library of Scotland; but such incorporations of photocopies as have been authorized, provided with appropriate warnings about ownership and use, will undoubtedly enhance even further the research value of the National Library's preeminent holdings of Scott correspondence. Even if photocopies are lent only for the use of the Survey rather than made part of National Library stock, registration will be all the more effective for the amicable exchange of cataloguing information: I hope other custodians will come to realize that we may have information to give as well as often rather burdensome requests to make. Ideally, personal inspection of the documents is most desirable; photocopies don't tell all. Apart from the pleasure and stimulation of working with originals instead of ghosts, there are watermarks, pencilled annotations, faint or doubtful readings to be checked, and all those cumulatively invaluable suggestions about provenance and associated papers which are the reward of intensive documentary analysis. Of course the dispersal of Scott's letters will make it impracticable to examine every one of them, but a thorough inspection of at least the principal collections will provide some useful insights into the physical side of his correspondence.

In a paper deliberately devoted mainly to collecting strategy and editorial techniques, I fear I am not going to have much time to speak of the literary content of the correspondence, which must be the principal justification of our work. So large an investment of official time and effort could not be defended if the quality of the material surveyed did not match its quantity. I am fully convinced that they are equal. Scott has never held a specially high reputation as a letter-writer; Carlyle's opinion that his letters "do not . . . proceed from the innermost parts of the mind"[5] has been influential. But self-revelation, as David Hewitt put it, "is not the only or even the proper measurement of the value or usefulness of correspondence,"[6] and even if one allows Carlyle's judgement to be true (I have many reservations) there are a number of levels on which the special value of Scott's letters can be appreciated.

Even if one says that Scott was not a great letter-writer, he was most certainly a great writer of letters, and his correspondence in all its bulk and variety offers us a remarkable autobiographical record of Scott the man, Scott the writer, and of his whole world. There is much, for example, on the study of antiquities, ballads and traditional verse; on the legal organization of Scotland, and the commercial world of contemporary publishing; on the development of Scott's estate at Abbotsford; and on local politics in Scotland and the Borders. Topics such as these - all of which have been illuminated by material turned up by the as yet underdeveloped Survey - are peripheral to his personal development and to his literary career as poet and novelist. I mention them to show how the correspondence provides us with a commentary upon the life and times of one of the leading and most intelligent men of the early nineteenth century.

Important new literary correspondences have been traced, for example that with Lady Douglas, his early friend and encourager who is known mainly from rather shadowy references in Lockhart's biography. There is an important group to Lady Anne Barnard, the author of "Auld Robin Gray," written to her late in her life but with all the spirited light-heartedness which a cultivated female correspondent was always able to call forth from Scott. Many other single letters of the first rank have newly come to light - to Scott's son Walter, or Richard Lovell Edgeworth about his daughter Maria, to take two examples from recent National Library acquisitions - which constantly elevate and justify the more humdrum tasks of recording lesser items. But perhaps even more important than these star pieces is the possibility of filling out sequences imperfectly represented in the Centenary Edition and the "Grierson rejects" (the supplementary typescript material), of piecing together a series of scattered letters and thus being able to show how apparently insignificant items acquire coherence once again when reassembled in a register.

Some of Scott's minor business letters, apparently merely of "autograph" interest singly, will take on something approaching life when grouped in this way. Among more important correspondents, it will be an interesting task to investigate Scott's correspondence with J.W. Croker, the civil servant, bibliophile and Tory propagandist, in the light of his letters in at least three repositories in New York (Morgan, Berg and Pforzheimer collections), at Yale and Ann Arbor, in private hands and at the National Library of Scotland. By concentrating the information in this way, the Survey will at last make such a study possible. I do not wish, however, to give further examples, as fresh possibilities are constantly suggesting themselves as work proceeds and new material comes to light: it is inevitable, and stimulating, that this should be so. In the nature of things the Survey will never be complete, and it would be idle to expect it. New documents will always be coming to light to tease the compilers, but it would be wrong to keep any proposed published checklist in a state of perpetual penultimation. At least by having a permanent and well-known centre at which information can be added, Scott studies in the future will gain efficiently from these inevitable addenda.

Surveying, registration, checklisting, all are ways of solving the problem which I outlined. The opportunity they present is an interesting and challenging one, particularly when it involves a great library in an unusual way, since previously this sort of work has more commonly been conducted in universities or by scholars working privately. Although I have stressed earlier that a new edition is not at present envisaged, and that it would be most inadvisable to consider it seriously until we know as fully as possible what may be involved, it might be worth also considering the additional opportunity which is offered by the present state of Scott's letters. For, even when the proposal is hedged about with every possible reservation, the possibility of producing a completely revised editon of the letters of Sir Walter Scott, incorporating all the traceable new material and correcting the older texts, must always be borne in mind. Such a plan gives shape and additional purpose to the enterprise of surveying the documents. Whether it will ever come about is, to put it mildly, and in a phrase beloved of the British civil service, open to doubt. Discussing the matter before so experienced (and productive) an audience as this at least gives me an opportunity of mentioning a few points which might be of more general interest.

I have tried to explain the inadequacies of the available text, and the amount of supplementary and corrective material of major literary and biographical significance. I may not have stressed enough the bulk, variety and importance of Scott's incoming correspondence, which enriches our understanding of his own letters to such an extent that at least selective (if not comprehensive) publication might be justified in an edition of correspondence rather than merely of letters. They would swell the bulk but the case for their inclusion would be a strong one. On the other hand, even the selective publication of incoming materials, which would in any case have to be examined closely for annotation, might swell the edition to an unacceptable size; it should never be forgotten that it is Scott's own letters rather than his two-sided correspondence which are the most important. Let us say, however, for the sake of argument, that a correspondence of twelve thousand items is available for consideration. Would a traditional letterpress publication in (say) forty volumes be justified? There would have to be an immense investment of money in editorial work; heavy administrative charges; transcription, annotation, and correction, typesetting and correction, indexing and correction: all would add their costs. There would be the delays inevitable in any project of this kind, aggravating the locking-up of later materials while the customarily desired chronological sequence is maintained in issuing the long series of volumes. Then there is publication itself: heaven knows what the retail price would have to be, even with every available grant and subsidy, were this massive scheme to reach the point of publication in (say) seven or ten years. Might we not have reached the stage now at which the conventional publication of a massive series of letters has quite passed the point at which it is financially practicable? I don't think this takes too gloomy a view of the current economics of epistolary editing.

How far can such a project be said to be academically desirable? A survey of the kind I have outlined, perhaps with adjustments to indicate more of the contents of the individual letters, gets scholars quite a long way on the road to comprehensive documentary coverage. The last twenty years have seen rapid changes in the techniques of photographic and electrostatic copying; the next decade will see many more. There has been an increasingly liberal policy on the part of holding institutions to make photocopies of their documents available to research, subject to restrictions on use which are usually but the codification of scholarly good manners. A substantial portion of the material surveyed and checklisted would therefore be available on request to interested parties prepared to take the trouble to apply to holding institutions. They would of course not have at their fingertips the annotation or the intensive indexing of an edition, but might not such additional benefits be regarded as jam on the buttered bread which modern photographic methods and library co-operation provide for a substantial part of the corpus of Scott's correspondence? They would also lack the benefit of having the texts transcribed; Scott's handwriting, notably at the end of his life and at a few shorter earlier periods, is difficult but not insuperable. And limitations on access to that part of the corpus privately owned, restrictively held or otherwise unavailable, are another objection. Even so, it might not entirely unreasonably be held that a sufficiently large representative selection of manuscript correspondence is within the reach of scholars to make the effort of editing it comprehensively a work of supererogation.

These are devil's-advocate arguments and I bring them out because they may be relevant to other large-scale scholarly projects which are threatened by rising costs, scholarly delays and a diminishing market. One possible solution which I have in mind may be equally naive, but I hope it may also have some general application. While electrostatic copying has gone ahead fast, microform publication has been de-veloping even quicker, microfiche succeeding microfilm and both achieving an increasingly high technical quality. Micro-form publishing is now almost at the point where individual reading equipment is cheap and efficient enough for it to secure scholarly acceptance. Recent improvements in photo-graphic techniques admit of more stringently controlled production standards, and there will certainly be further improvements in the next decade, which may see the breaching of that all-important barrier of full acceptance by the aca-demic community, including scholarly publishers and literary editors and reviewers. Should we not therefore be looking ahead to a point where, with traditional processes obsolescent and beyond price for scholarly publication on so vast a scale, these new techniques might provide the only solution to the problem of issuing a comprehensive text of Scott's letters within a reasonable time and at a bearable price?

Might there not be something to be said for a high quality typescript containing a transcription of certifiably high standard and basic but not exhaustive annotation and apparatus, together with a full index - all available in microform (microfiche being my personal preference against microfilm)? This would surely satisfy most of our learned requirements, providing a basic and comprehensive working text for which (as I said earlier) confirmatory photocopies of many of the items would be available from public collections. The palaeographical problems already mentioned, general aesthetic criteria, and the greater degree of visual and intellectual control which type or typescript affords, all emphasize that a transcription would be vastly preferable to the reproduction of original manuscripts, another possibility which might be considered for more consistently legible texts.

The result, even when made as attractive and accessible as the form admits, would be very much an accumulation of learning that will appeal only to specialists amongst the learned community. It would not be a popular publication in any sense, but a serviceable tool of scholarship, providing a rich source. Micropublication would make it seem more difficult and unapproachable than it actually is, but similar charges could be laid against many shelves of multi-volume editions of correspondence which it is misleading to think of as delightful repositories of readily accessible literature. The interest of the general reader can and should be borne in mind when such epistolary behemoths are conceived (and "general reader" must nowadays embrace the critical literary student whose demands or stamina do not extend to comprehensive editions of correspondence). *Editiones minores* could be quarried from the greater accumulation with a skill and judgement which might well attract a readership even beyond literary students; and the full quarry remains for the critical, biographical and thematic investigation of Scott's life and times with a documentary thoroughness and confidence never before achievable. I therefore put forward a scheme of thorough registration, comprehensive publication and selective popularization as an opportunity currently available in Scott studies which may possibly have interesting applications for other subjects.

This notion of microfiche (or microform) publication which I have outlined for Scott may be applicable to other large-scale textual series, and the rationale - saving of editorial time, limitation of costs, speed of production, etc. - is one which all potential editors of correspondence might do well to consider before they start. It has already been put into effect for a microfiche edition of the papers of the eighteenth-century American architect Benjamin Henry Latrobe, a size-able task involving 315 microfiche cards, containing some twelve thousand exposures with supporting indexes, and a selective letterpress edition also in mind.[7] With Latrobe the reproduction of sketchbooks and architectural drawings makes the medium particularly appropriate. The editor, Edward C. Carter II of the Maryland Historical Society, who presented an impressive report on his work to the annual conference of the Society of American Archivists in 1976, was then at pains to point out that quality microform editing is not cheap - it requires the solid intellectual commitment and the same high textual skills which conventional publication would demand. (This is an important point: the similarity of care and effort needed for book-form or microform publication may be why scholars have stuck to the former for so long. By the time the preparation of the text has been completed it may usually have seemed worth-while to finish the job in full size.)

Another microfiche edition now under way is that which the Voltaire Foundation has recently announced: a transcribed and annotated text of the ten thousand letters forming the incoming literary and political correspondence of Pierre Michel Hennin, the eighteenth-century French diplomatist, which is being prepared by Michael L. Berkvam and Peter L. Smith: four hundred microfiches (with printed volumes of introductions, lists and indexes to complement them) packing into eight binders something which might have matched Theodore Besterman's own definitive edition of Voltaire's correspondence in size - and exceeded it in price. Editions on this scale and with the backing of organizations like the Maryland Historical Society and the Voltaire Foundation will undoubtedly help to ensure the technological and bibliographical acceptance of similar projects in the future.

Surely this is the direction in which editors of correspondence should be looking in future. One vast undertaking that will have to be considered some day, which in scale and technique may be comparable with Scott, is a full edition of Ruskin's letters. He is not a letter-writer I know much about, but the problems seem to be rather similar: a wide scattering of manuscripts with several accessible concentrations; a bulky and reputable but far from comprehensive basic edition, supplemented by several recent volumes of individual correspondences well edited; and the increased availability of innumerable unpublished and uncollected smaller groups. There may be all sorts of tactical variations between Scott and Ruskin, but many of the problems of research in the confused world (at least to outsiders) of Ruskin's correspondence could be solved by checklisting, and the registration might even be followed by a revised-text microform edition, annotated as appropriate and well indexed. I may have chosen Ruskin unwisely as an example, but amongst other interested scholars my friend Dr. John Dixon Hunt, who is preparing a new biography of Ruskin based on comprehensive documentary research, has told me that he feels I am thinking along the right lines, but emphasizes against the luxury of a microform text the more urgent need for a first-rate checklist which could be updated. Perhaps, he suggests, a computer might be used - an application which, out of a mixture of apprehensiveness and incomprehension, I have refrained from urging here for Scott. The Survey seems manageable without elaborate mechanization, but an edition would be an obvious candidate for the application of computer techniques.

So far I have spoken of applying microform methods to large-scale ventures, but they might also be considered for lesser projects where the quality or quantity of material may not justify full conventional publication in the present climate of academic finance, but which it would nevertheless be highly satisfactory to have published by other means. Take James Hogg, the Ettrick Shepherd, for example. Following the successful inauguration of the Scott Survey, a number of Hogg scholars based on the University of Stirling have been preparing a compararable checklist of Hogg letters and manu-scripts. The market would have to be a strong one to support a letterpress edition of his correspondence, but an edition in microform might well be thought a feasible extension of the fruitful work of Mr. Douglas Mack and his fellow-compilers. To take another Scottish example, there is Henry Cockburn, Lord Cockburn, the early nineteenth-century Scottish judge and autobiographer. His letters (I have over the years tran-scribed some seven hundred of them) are long, delightful, witty, sharp and informative, a first-rate social, legal and literary source. Even with Professor Karl Miller's award-winning study *Cockburn's Millennium*[8] to introduce them to a world less knowledgeable of the great Edinburgh legal memorialist than they should be, I am not sure whether a complete edition would be practicable. A selection certainly would be, and I hope it might eventually take shape, possibly alongside a more comprehensive text in the form I have been discussing for Scott and others.

Much of what I have been saying is tentative; some of it may be thought - in the presence of so many distinguished editors - to be unduly tendentious. If some of it succeeds in provoking the sort of discussion which this celebrated series of Toronto editorial conferences should be able to call forth, I am sure that I for one will have a lot to learn.

NOTES

1 *The Letters of Sydney Smith*, ed. Nowell C. Smith, Oxford, Clarendon Press, 1953, 2 vols.
2 D.S. Hewitt, "What should we do about Scott's letters?" *Scottish Literary News*, 2 (1971), 3-10.
3 Even an American reprint, by the AMS Company, has not helped accessibility, especially in Great Britain.
4 H.J.C. Grierson, *Sir Walter Scott, Bart.*, London, Constable, 1938.
5 Thomas Carlyle, *Critical and Miscellaneous Essays*, London, Chapman and Hall, 1899, IV, p. 61.
6 D.S. Hewitt, *op. cit.*, p. 3.
7 The microtext edition is announced by the James T. White Company, Clifton, N.J.
8 Karl Miller, *Cockburn's Millennium*, London, Duckworth, 1975.

The Hunt for
the Disraeli Letters

John Matthews

"First," said Mrs. Beeton, "catch your rabbit." Editors of correspondence know well the futility of this advice. Few indeed have the security of knowing, when they begin, the exact dimensions of the material they will be editing - and this uncertainty - the hope that a new and unexpected cache of letters of enormous importance lies in the next attic - is part of the joy of the enterprise. But I would submit to you that while I know each of us is convinced that his own special rabbit has qualities belonging to no other, the case of the Disraeli letters does introduce a problem of scale. In the early days so much new material kept coming in, that editing seemed more like Alice's game of croquet than anything else.

Donald Schurman and I made a joint application for a Killam award in 1971, just before we were both due to go to England on sabbatical leave for 1972-73. We were not successful, being told, at the interview, fairly politely, that our proposal (I was going to prepare an edition of Disraeli's letters, and Schurman a companion collection of his speeches), had been rejected, because everything worth knowing about Disraeli was already known, and most of his letters had already been published.

We went ahead anyway. I was convinced that there was a place for a really complete edition of Disraeli's letters, and within the limits of those known to have survived, the task did not seem an overwhelming one. After all, as the Killam people had said, the locations were known and listed; but there were known to be serious deficiencies in the accuracy of the texts which had been presented in the editions of letters edited by Disraeli's brother Ralph in the 1880s,[1] although most of the originals from which he drew seemed not to have survived, and so could not be checked. Monypenny, and, to a lesser extent, Buckle, drew heavily on Ralph's texts, and on the dating which he had assigned to the letters, in the preparation of their monumental biography.[2]

Scholars, for a long time, have been pointing out the value of an accurate and complete edition of Disraeli's letters. As early as 1882, the year after Disraeli's death, Sir Philip Rose wrote to Lord Rowton:

> If we should be so fortunate as to discover Lord B's letters to his family in reply to theirs, which no doubt were preserved, a work of the rarest interest can be compiled, which will exhibit the inner life of our friend to the world, in a light which even his most devoted friends can have no notion.[3]

He was, of course, speaking more accurately than he knew, and in ways other than perhaps he meant; but all subsequent biographers have commented on the indispensability of Disraeli's letters as primary sources for all facets of his complex life and personality, and have regretted the absence of a complete collection.

Robert Blake, now a member of our Board, had his own words brought back to him when he attended the Disraeli Colloquium last April at Queen's as the keynote speaker. In the preface to his *Disraeli* in 1967 he had stressed this need:

> All subsequent writers about Disraeli must acknowledge their debt to Monypenny and Buckle. Perhaps some day some wealthy foundation will finance a complete edition of the correspondence of the best letter-writer among all English statesmen. Till that day the official biography remains the nearest.[4]

Much later in his biography, Lord Blake pays a further tribute, almost uncharacteristically lyrical, about the quality of the letters and of their value to both historians and literary scholars:

> Disraeli's letters give a picture of his whole way of life, and, as with his novels, indeed with everything he wrote, there is a sparkle, movement and vivacity which never fail to entrance. His prose when not rococo and ornate - and in his letters it seldom is - has the swift quality of sunshine seen through moving leaves or tumbling waters. The crisp freshness is there even when he is describing events of a character anything but sunny. (p. 418)

This special quality of the letters is emphasized because it forms the basis for our decision to undertake a complete rather than a selected edition. With many writers it is a simple matter to separate the "important" letters from the trivial ones, the domestic, the dutiful. With Disraeli it is not. To each of his correspondents he sees himself in a role which he projects - always different with each one - developing and changing as his own life does. It is when these letters are collected in chronological order that one becomes aware for the first time of the complexity of a personality in which the sum is greater than and different from the parts. All of Disraeli's more eminent biographers have been aware of this special quality, and hence their testimony to the need for a collection as complete as possible in order to reveal it.

There are very few letters, therefore, which, when placed in context can be called trivial - very few dutiful bread-and-butter letters which do not go beyond their original motivation and achieve their own importance in the mosaic.

In 1972, then, the prospects seemed set fair for a rapid garnering of the known collections, with the hope that there might be as many as several hundred more to be uncovered on the periphery. Queen's had generously made it possible financially for me to obtain the whole of the Hughenden Archives[5] on microfilm, and, after poring over portions of that, and using Oxford as a base, I began timidly to make sorties. The first was to Weston Park in Shropshire, where Lord Bradford was generous enough to give me free access to his archives. You may remember that Disraeli's letters to the sisters, Selina, Lady Bradford, and Anne, Lady Chesterfield, give what has been the most comprehensive and detailed personal portrait of Disraeli during his second ministry, between 1874 and 1880. Buckle printed 450 of them in the last two volumes of the biography.[6] But it soon became obvious that on his visits to Weston in 1918-19, Buckle had not been shown the complete collection. Even Lord Zetland's 1929 edition, though considerably more comprehensive, was not complete.[7] The reason, of course, is perhaps obvious enough, but it was to be repeated over and over again with all the major listed collections. Disraeli was completely uninhibited in his private correspondence; he said exactly what he thought about everybody, with his character assessments supported by a flood of anecdote filled with graphic detail. In the early part of this century many of the subjects were still alive, and would have been extremely upset, not to say litigious. After another fifty years, however, attitudes have changed, and no obstacles are offered either by the descendants of those of whom Disraeli wrote or by the owners of the letters. But, to my surprise, believing a particular collection to have been thoroughly mined by a respected and reliable predecessor, many scholars have not bothered to go back to the originals, and those that have seem not to have realized the proportion of new and unpublished materials which are there.

In every case, the known collections proved to be larger than had been expected, and of course, in most cases the new material was more lively than the old. The archives at Weston, Hughenden, Nottingham, the letters to Mrs. Brydges-Willyams and to Lady Londonderry, all yielded more than had been expected.

Then there were the hitherto unknown collections. In most cases these were found by tracing the descendants of Disraeli's known correspondents. In Hughenden alone there are about fifty people who wrote to Disraeli who are classed as major correspondents, and over 1,100 in the general correspondence lists. The peers were the first to be tackled, as their descendants were easier to find, and then all the rest of the general list, with careful examination of their letters to Disraeli in the hope that they would provide enough clues to their identities to permit their descendants to be traced.

Belvoir Castle proved to be a rich source, particularly for the 1840s and the Young England movement, but there were also some letters from the 1830s. Many peers did not know what they had. The Dukes of Abercorn, Newcastle, Argyle, and Richmond and Gordon, all had holdings of which they were not precisely aware - and which testify how thoroughly Disraeli had made up for his father's comment after the publication of *The Young Duke* in 1831: "What does Ben know of Dukes?"

The correspondence to William Pyne, the man who, more than any other, kept Disraeli out of gaol in the 1830s, turned up, not then catalogued, in the Fitzwilliam Museum in Cambridge. The Bodleian, in addition to its known holdings, had the private deposit collections of Lord Carrington and Lord Harcourt, and it was only by the sheerest accident that I encountered this (to me) hitherto quite unknown category of archival collection - the one which, without direct reference to the repository by the owner, does not officially exist. Ashamed of my ignorance, I have been comforted a little by discovering that many of my much more experienced and knowledgeable colleagues did not know of it either. At first I had been afraid that these collections might exist in all the county record offices and libraries which I had already laboriously solicited; however it appears that they only survive at the Bodleian and at the British Library (where for example, a Portland private deposit collection is kept). While the present Earl of Derby has been most co-operative with the papers in his possession, including those of the 14th and 15th Earls, the whereabouts of those of the 16th (the one immortalized in the Canadian Stanley Cup), remain a mystery, unknown to the present family or its collaterals. I suspect a private deposit collection, but until I can find the owner there is no way to know.

You may remember that Lord Esher reported in 1905 that Disraeli's personal correspondence with Queen Victoria had been destroyed on the order of Edward VII. No one had any reason to question this, and it has been generally accepted, appearing again as recently as in Cecil Woodham-Smith's biography of Victoria.[8] Yet as more and more of the correspondence from the 1870s came to light, the more uncharacteristic such an action on the King's part appeared to be. Relations between Disraeli and the Prince were extremely warm, and additional evidence emerged of the number of occasions on which Disraelian diplomacy was exercised successfully with the Queen on the Prince's behalf. Besides, Edward did not share his sister Beatrice's habits with archives. Through the good offices of the Royal Archivist, Sir Robin Mackworth Young, and by gracious permission of Her Majesty, we now have on microfilm a complete collection of both sides of the correspondence between Disraeli and Queen Victoria, the great majority of which has not been published, drawn from the Royal Archives and from the Personal Archives. This bears all the marks of a "personal correspondence," and whether or not other letters were destroyed over seventy years ago, enough remains to justify the claim that a personal correspondence has indeed survived.

It is a commonplace to say that Disraeli's letters to women always have special quality, and that he needed a female correspondent for his confidante. We have now his letters to his sister Sarah, to his wife Mary Anne, Lady Londonderry, Mrs. Brydges-Willyams, Hannah Rothschild, Lady Blessington, the Sheridan sisters, Lady John Manners, Lady Bradford, Lady Chesterfield, the Queen, and dozens of others. Disraeli's letters to women managed to achieve a tone of almost instant intimacy, and during this hunt I have come across a number of cases where Disraeli would write to one of his female correspondents who, in every instance, cherished the letters and preserved them carefully. Upon her death, the immediate family would find them, read them, be horrified at the implications of their familiarity of tone, and destroy them: each time, alas verified, Disraeli and his correspondent had not even met.

During a search of this type one encounters a wide range of family legends to account for the apparent absence of papers which one might reasonably have expected to have survived. These range from explosion, terrorism (in Ireland), enemy action, accident, and assorted forms of both mayhem and inadvertence. By far the most common, however, was a variation on the Carlyle theme - either an ignorant housemaid or an inebriated footman (invariably one or the other) is reported to have destroyed archives containing Disraeli letters, always by fire, and always between 1901 and 1911. This happened so often that I have come to suspect the growth of a racial myth - perhaps designed intuitively as an unanswerable defence against the obduracy of North American research enquiries. Either that, or a tendency of considerable, if as yet unreported, significance involved the domestic servants in Edwardian country houses in a wave of uncontrollable arson.

Credence is given to this theory by the location of three collections that were alleged to have met this fate. The Drunken Footman cases, therefore, are in a special category, and we have not given up on them, as we were tempted to do at the beginning.

While it is a source of no little satisfaction to have located a collection after laboriously piecing clues together, it is a more mixed experience to encounter letters unexpectedly. I visited a country house recently in a very remote area of Britain, owned by a family with no Disraeli connections, purely as a tourist, because it had been newly opened to the public. Without any expectations at all, but with that compulsion which my colleagues will recognize, I asked the Steward about Disraeli letters. To my astonishment there was a sizeable collection, one which I had been looking for with decreasing hope, and whose location in this place bore a provenance that one could only describe as clouded. This element of the random educes melancholy thoughts. How many more such caches are there? Should one knock on every third door of the kingdom, exhorting the occupants to bring out their Disraeli letters?

As an aside, I should add that I have been struck by the large number of Palmerston letters which I have encountered during this search, and the prospects look most encouraging for anyone who does not have enough editorial problems of his own, and who would like to acquire new ones with a Palmerston project. In some places it was necessary to sweep away the Palmerston letters before one could get at the Disraeli ones.

Chance aside, the usual way of trying to make a broader sweep than is possible from specific enquiries is through press advertisements. We used this, of course, with the customary notices in *The Times, T.L.S.* and several other British newspapers and periodicals. The results have been for us disappointing. Fewer than twenty letters have come to us through this means. A much more fruitful source has been the Curator of Hughenden Manor, who has been an invaluable friend and ally to us. He keeps a store of our propaganda displayed at the House, and through talking to many of the visitors has located a large number of small holdings of letters I am sure we would not otherwise have found. This is mainly because, not content with leaving them to write to us, he takes names and addresses on the spot and sends them to us to follow up. Mrs. Barbara North, of the National Trust Office, in charge of the Disraeli Archives at Hughenden, has been another invaluable ally, passing on to us contacts from all over the world who have made enquiry at her office.

One striking, if gloomy, consequence of the search as it has progressed over the last six years, has been the rapidly escalating price of Disraeliana in the marketplace. All editors, I suppose, have experienced this, and it appears inevitable, when it becomes known that there is a demand, for the price to go up. We may have merely coincided with the widespread rediscovery of Victoriana, but when one compares the present level of prices for Disraeli as opposed to, for example, Gladstone material, the charge that we have helped to drive them up is hard to avoid. Owners in general have been extremely open and co-operative; it is only recently, with letters fetching £250 that would not have brought £25 ten years ago, that we have begun to encounter owners who tell us they will not let us have copies, but that they are willing to negotiate a sale if we are interested.

Having finally located, for example, the originals of the so-called Home Letters of 1830-31, we were faced with this response. The collection was of such importance to the early period that we had little option but to buy them, although, obviously, we are not in the business of collecting manuscripts, but of processing texts. Where we encounter this for less important individual letters, we have to decide whether we are justified in buying the letter or whether we should try to keep track of it in the hope the next owner will permit us to have a photocopy of it.

The Jewish Museum collection provided a further unexpected example. The National Register of Archives listing for this collection gave no details of its size or scope. In 1973 I spent some days in the Jewish Museum in London cataloguing and listing the details of the Disraeli materials held there. When the job was finished, I left the original of the lists with the Secretary and asked for photocopies, which he agreed to have made and sent to me. The next communication was a notice of a decision of the Board of the Museum, which appeared to indicate that they had not known how much Disraeli material they had, and now that they did, they intended to sell it. As provision of copies, they added, might decrease the value of the manuscripts, they declined to provide them. The collection was promptly sent to Sotheby's, and it began to be sold, little by little, from 1974 on. The whole collection still has not been entirely disposed of, but we have had to keep tabs on each item, try to trace the purchaser, and then ask for photocopies. In most cases we have been successful, but it has been a very trying process.

The first volume of letters, up to the end of 1834, is now in at the Press, and the second, 1835-37, should be safely lodged before Christmas.[9] In addition to all the letters published for the first time, we have located most of those on which Ralph Disraeli drew for his editions. These too, we think, should be given the status of letters published for the first time, for although it has been widely known that his texts were suspect, it may now be seen what an extraordinarily unreliable source they have been for any historical research on Disraeli's early career. Time after time we have encountered in his text letters conflated from parts of as many as five originals (sometimes years apart), sometimes given the date of one of the parts, and sometimes assigned a date belonging to none of them.[10] Words and sentences have been changed and rewritten; sometimes meanings have been reversed. In the publication history section of the headnote for each of these letters, we have indicated which pieces of it Ralph used for his tapestry, so that the reader may realize how high a proportion of each letter is newly printed.

As we begin to go to press, we are very conscious of our failures. There are still so many gaps we had hoped to fill. We have not found Disraeli's letters to Lord Chandos, or to Lord George Bentinck. We had not really expected to find those to Henrietta Sykes, but there was a residual hope not quite extinguished. There are 248 original letters bound in to an extra-illustrated set of Monypenny and Buckle's biography which was sold in London in 1921 to a Mr. Cazenove, but in spite of every effort to trace the set and the purchaser, we have not yet succeeded. They are no doubt on someone's shelf awaiting some chance discovery. But with so much to do, we cannot wait. We intend to publish a supplementary volume or volumes, after the chronological publication is over, to contain all those that have emerged too late for their inclusion in the correct chronological sequence.

If there is a moral to be drawn from all this, it is an encouraging one: even with the better-known authors the work is never all done; there is always a great deal more to be known. The woods are still full of treasure, and attics still hold their burdens of forgotten papers.

NOTES

1 Ralph Disraeli ed., *Home Letters written by the late Earl of Beaconsfield in 1830 and 1831,* London, John Murray, 1885. Ralph Disraeli ed., *Lord Beaconsfield's Correspondence with his Sister, 1832-1852,* London, John Murray, 1886. Ralph Disraeli ed., *Lord Beaconsfield's Letters, 1830-1852,* London, John Murray, 1887.

2 William Flavelle Monypenny and George Earle Buckle, *The Life of Benjamin Disraeli, Earl of Beaconsfield,* 6 vols., London, John Murray, 1910-20. The two were not co-authors. Monypenny died after completing the first two volumes, and Buckle succeeded him as official biographer through appointment by the Beaconsfield Trust.

3 Memorandum of 1 September 1882, Rose Papers, Hughenden Archives, Box 308.

4 Robert Blake, *Disraeli,* New York, St. Martin's Press, 1967, p. xxi.

5 In late 1978 the Hughenden Archives were transferred by the National Trust to the Bodleian Library, Oxford. The Hughenden numbering system is, fortunately, to be maintained.

6 Volumes V and VI, by Buckle, were both published in 1920.

7 The Marquis of Zetland ed., *The Letters of Disraeli to Lady Bradford and Lady Chesterfield,* 2 vols., London, Ernest Benn, 1929.

8 Cecil Woodham-Smith, *Queen Victoria,* I, London, Hamish Hamilton, 1972.

9 The texts were lodged on schedule, and the first two volumes, to be published together, should appear during 1979.

10 As one example, in his 1886 volume (pp. 64-66), Ralph Disraeli printed a composite letter dated "May 1837" which was made up of extracts from 1837 letters dated 17 April, 26 April, 17 May, 12 June, 15 June and 10 August.

Editing Zola's Correspondence: When is a Letter not a Letter?

John A. Walker

When I became a member of the Zola Correspondence Project team,[1] I was totally without experience in the business of editing correspondences. Consequently I brought with me some rather strange ideas. For example, I thought I knew what a correspondence is. I thought it was definable as a group of letters. Worse still, I thought I knew what a letter is. If someone had thought to ask me for a definition, I would have said, recklessly, that a letter is a written message sent by one person to another person. Maybe if I had been urged, I might have added what every secondary-school student is taught, or used to be taught: that a letter generally has a distinct and recognizable form - dateline; opening salutation; message; the concluding salutation (which used to be rather long in English letters and still is long in some French letters); and signature. But I don't really think I'd have gone into that without being urged. I would have been

content with the person-to-person written-message definition.
And I thought I knew that a correspondence was a group of
such messages.

That is how naïve I was. Of course, my naïveté was not
totally ridiculous. The things I thought I knew have turned
out to be reasonably valid, my definitions have proved to
be reasonably accurate, for the great majority of the Zola
letters we shall publish. But not for all. My definition of a
letter was adequate for most cases; but editors of correspondences are responsible for *all* cases.

It was not long before I was made aware of this. Among
the first batch of Zola letters which were turned over to me
for annotation, there was one addressed to a two-man team
of novelists, Raoul Vast and Georges Ricouard, who had sent
Zola the pre-publication proofs of their latest novel, *Madame
Bécart,*[2] and had asked him for an opinion. Nothing unusual
there: it was 1879, Zola had recently had his first important
success as a novelist with *L'Assommoir,* he was now a well-
known literary figure, and young writers were frequently
appealing to him for advice and help. Zola remembered the
hard days before his first success, and was generous with
advice and help. In this case, he had written back to Vast
and Ricouard with a short but incisive evaluation of their
novel. We possessed a photocopy of the manuscript of
Zola's letter, and so there were no problems that I could see.
I did my annotations and turned them in to our chief editor,
Bard Bakker, with the rest of the letters.

A few days later Bard Bakker called me into his office. He
was looking at the letter in question, having separated it from
the rest of the batch. He thought there was something irregular
about this one: there were too many variants. I promptly
produced the photocopy of the original, to demonstrate that
the variants were authentic. Bakker thereupon suggested that
I consider all the other letters I had turned in, and asked
whether there was a single one with even half as many

variants.

I had to acknowledge that there was not. This letter was different. Zola was normally a very courteous and conscientious correspondent. He wrote legibly, he dated almost all his letters, and what is even more improbable, he almost always dated them correctly; and above all, he did not send messy letters with numerous crossings-out and corrections between the lines or in the margins. And the result is that, in his ordinary person-to-person written messages, variants are rare. So that when one comes across a letter containing a substantial number of textual changes, the experienced editor of Zola hears a bell ring. Bard Bakker had heard it immediately; I, being inexperienced, had not. Bakker suggested that, in order to acquire some experience as quickly as possible, I should try making a few comparisons. I might compare the letter in question with other manuscript letters, and then go on to compare it with some other Zola manuscripts in our collection - sketches, plans, working papers, manuscripts of novels; in general, texts whose final purpose was to produce something for publication. I did so, and began to hear the bell. One hardly even needed to read the pages; it was enough to look at them. The appearance of the pages made the difference clear. The manuscript of the letter to Vast and Ricouard did not *look* like the manuscript of a letter, but like that of a text written for publication. Words and phrases scratched out, words and phrases added between the lines and in the margins: all the things that Zola the courteous correspondent refrained from doing in his letters, all the things that Zola the professional writer regularly did in the texts whose purpose was publication, were visibly present in the manuscript of the letter.

At that point I decided that I had to know whether Zola really had written the letter for publication or not. The novel about which he had written to Vast and Ricouard was, to put it mildly, obscure; but the title did appear in the catalogue of the Bibliothèque Nationale. There had been one edition, and only one, after which the work had been consigned to oblivion. When I finally had a chance to read the novel during a visit to Paris, I decided that the oblivion was richly deserved. But in the volume which contained this egregiously forgettable novel by two fortunately forgotten novelists, there appeared also a text which must certainly be rescued from oblivion, because it was signed by Emile Zola. It was of course the text of my letter. Zola had indeed written it for publication, and it had indeed been published as a preface to the novel. Or rather, more precisely, a letter-preface, since it was published *in toto*, complete with dateline, salutation, message, closing formula, and signature. A letter, and yet not a letter; because it was also, and more importantly, a preface.

Furthermore, since it was a preface written by Zola to be published with a novel by a pair of relatively unknown writers, it was also, and perhaps most important of all, yet another thing: an advertisement. Zola was not helping the two young writers solely, or even primarily, with advice. That letter was a commercial message. From the time of his success with *L'Assommoir* in 1877, Zola was, and knew he was, not only a well-known writer who sold a lot of copies of his own books; he was also a public figure, a controversial personage whose name was regularly appearing in the columns (including the gossip columns) of the Parisian dailies, whose face and figure were constantly being caricatured in the newspapers, and whose every written word had value in the literary marketplace. A letter-preface signed by Zola was like an iron-clad guarantee of improved sales. And Zola knew it. He had spent years of his life (1862 to 1866) working in the publicity department at Hachette, and he knew about selling books. More than a letter, more than a preface, that text was also, and primarily, an advertisement.

Does one publish advertisements in an edition of a correspondence? There could be no doubt that the text ought to be published. Not just because Zola has in our day acquired a prestige such that every word he ever wrote is considered publishable, but because the text in question contained some opinions of Zola on specifically literary matters. The question was not whether the text should be published; it was whether we ought to consider that text as a letter, like other letters, to be published side by side with texts which were indisputably, and purely, letters. And the question was important because this particular letter-preface-advertisement represents a whole category of texts which raised questions about what is suitable for publication in a correspondence. A question of principle was involved, and we who were responsible for the edition were going to have to find an answer which at the very least would serve as a guideline. Even if in certain cases we might make an *ad hoc* decision in contravention of a principle, we needed to establish the principle.

It was not long before my naïveté was damaged again. As I worked my way through my second assignment of Zola letters, I reached a point in the 1880 batch at which Zola became embroiled in a particularly acrimonious and juicy literary-political dispute with Jules Laffitte, the editor of the daily *Le Voltaire,* where Zola had been a regular columnist for several years. The editorial position of the journal was solid middle-of-the-road support of the existing bourgeois-republican regime. But Zola's opinions, as published in *Le Voltaire,* were becoming more and more vituperatively hostile to men and institutions which he saw as deliberately impeding progress toward social justice. Laffitte didn't want to lose a columnist whose name sold a lot of papers, but Laffitte's political friends finally decided that Zola was going too far, and Laffitte was obliged to publish an article dissociating himself and the entire staff of *Le Voltaire* from the opinions Zola had been publishing on the front page of that newspaper. Such an article was understood as a notice of separation. Zola promptly sent Laffitte a message which was not in the form of an article, since he knew that henceforth his articles would no longer appear in *Le Voltaire;* the text was in the form of a letter to Laffitte. We do not have the manuscript version of that letter, but the content makes it entirely clear that the letter was written to be published: in it, Zola continues the political polemic which had been appearing in his articles, and he takes public leave of the readers who had been following his columns in *Le Voltaire* for several years.[3]

Now this letter to Laffitte, and Zola's subsequent letters continuing the public debate, belong to another category which raises questions, some of which are similar to the questions raised by the letter-prefaces, some of which are different. The texts again have the form of letters; but do they have the content? One might want to attribute them to the special and clearly definable category of letters to the editor (or, a little more broadly, open letters); but this is not entirely satisfactory either, since the messages contained in these letters are a continuation of the polemics in previously published texts which were not letters at all, but newspaper articles.

For this category, as for the letter-preface category, there is no argument about whether the texts ought to be published. The question is whether it is our responsibility to publish them as part of the edition of the Zola correspondence. If they are a continuation of the polemics in the published articles, are they letters? Would it not be more suitable to publish them with the articles?

Furthermore, in addition to these questions of principle, there were some practical considerations which we had to face. When we began preparing our edition, we knew of the existence of about 2,500 letters written by Zola. We also knew, of course, that there were other letters waiting to be discovered or revealed; but we underestimated how many. We are now certain of the existence of more than 4,000 letters, and there is no reason to believe that we are anywhere near the end. Our first volume, which appeared in November of 1978, was already much thicker, and much more expensive, than we had hoped. One cannot help being tempted at times by the thought that we might achieve some reduction in the size and price of the volumes if we simply decided to exclude letter-prefaces, letters to the editor, open letters, and other such doubtful categories. Couldn't somebody else do these special cases, as part of a different editorial enterprise? Some of the texts might even appear sooner that way, for our present plans call for our edition to be completed in 1992 .... Dare we think such thoughts?

Not all the members of the team are prepared to dare. I don't always dare myself. But there are some cases in which I do; and in these cases I may yet find myself in serious disagreement with some of my colleagues. One very special case in particular: one of the most famous, and arguably one of the most important texts Zola ever wrote, is in the form of a letter - an open letter, which was intended for publication, and was indeed published, and which (it is here that I ask the question about the need for publication in our correspondence) has been republished innumerable times in innumerable places. I mean of course the letter which was published under the title *J'accuse,* as if it were a newspaper article; but it is known that the title was Clemenceau's idea, not Zola's, and that Zola had written as his title "Open Letter to the President of the Republic."[4]

Now what do we do about *J'accuse?* Of course I respect and honour Zola for writing that dangerous text and publishing it over his own name; yet I still feel that it does not make sense to add to the size of our volume by publishing yet again a text which has often been published before and which, by its length and by its content, must be categorized as being primarily a polemical article. On the other hand, my colleague Henri Mitterand[5] is rather in favour of publishing all the open letters; he writes, in his preface to our edition (the translation is mine):

> Personally I have nothing against the inclusion of all of
> Zola's open letters in an edition of the *Correspondance;*
> these letters simply carry to their limits the models of
> content and style found in the private letters. They are
> addressed, through the medium of the newspaper, to the
> people of France as a collectivity; it is not an essential
> characteristic of a letter that it should be addressed to a
> single person. And if Zola's letters, as a literary genre,
> have any originality, any esthetic importance, any right
> to be known to posterity, it is because of the qualities
> of the letters he addressed to the public.[6]

Clearly Mitterand didn't intend to take a hard line in our
debates about what to include and what to exclude; he had
his arguments ready, but he was also ready to discuss. Now it
seemed to me that I ought to be prepared, when the debates
began, to discuss not only on the basis of principle, and not
only on the basis of practical considerations such as weight
and price, but also on the basis of another consideration
which might very well be perceived as important: the practices
already established by some of our predecessors in the area of
editing correspondences. The time I had at my disposal to
investigate past practices would, in an ideal world, have been
infinite; in the real world it was of course limited. Much as I
should have liked to spend months and years reading correspondences of different writers from different times and
places, I was forced to examine a corpus which, in relation to
the total available material, was severely limited. I decided
reluctantly that I would have to limit myself to correspondences of nineteenth-century French writers, because that
was our field.

In that field we are following in a particularly distinguished
tradition. In the preface from which I quoted above, Mitterand

mentions five important editions which have been or are being done of nineteenth-century French correspondences. They are those of Sainte-Beuve, by Jean Bonnerot;[7] of Mérimée, by Maurice Parturier;[8] of Balzac, by Roger Pierrot;[9] of George Sand, by Georges Lubin;[10] and of Flaubert, by Jean Bruneau.[11] I plunged into these editions, with the aim of discovering what principles and/or practices had guided our predecessors in making decisions about what is to be considered a letter and what is not, or what belongs in a correspondence and what does not.

My first discovery was not directly related to the problem which is the subject of this paper, but I am sure it is of interest in the context of the present conference, and I take the liberty of reporting it here. It is that the literary and linguistic qualities of these correspondences are of such importance that the texts should be on the programmes of our courses much more frequently than they are - and not only at the graduate level, but also in advanced undergraduate programmes. We are cheating our students, graduate and undergraduate, if we fail to make them aware of the values inherent in these texts. We are depriving them not only of the "pleasure of the text," although that is itself serious enough. We are also depriving them of biographical information that is at least as pertinent as anything they can find in official biographies. We are depriving them of an important part of their cultural heritage: the art of letter-writing, which the telephone is destroying; and we are thereby depriving them of the chance to study linguistic and semiotic procedures which are threatened with extinction. And we are depriving them of the chance to acquire excellent documentation on the thinking of nineteenth-century intellectuals about literature, politics, religion, love and sex.[12] Our students ought to be reading these texts.

But I had a more specific assignment in mind. I was searching these editions for precedents which could help the members of the Zola Correspondence Project to make decisions about what is and is not a letter. Naturally, each of the five distinguished editions which I examined in detail dealt in a different way with the questions that concern us, and each of these ways was determined partly by the characteristics of the writer of the correspondence, partly by criteria which the editor had established, and partly by various other considerations which I shall discuss.

Parturier's edition of the Mérimée correspondence is the one which limits itself most severely to texts which clearly belong to the category of person-to-person written messages and cannot be related to any other category. Certain characteristics of Mérimée contributed to the editor's decision.[13] Of the five writers whose correspondences I studied closely, Mérimée was the least committed to writing as either a profession or a vocation. Literature for him, much more than for the others, was an avocation. His more serious commitments were to his government job in art and archaeology, and to the pleasures of Parisian life as they were enjoyed by the prosperous bourgeoisie.[14] If there are in the Mérimée correspondence any texts whose status as letters might possibly be questioned, they are the interminable reports Mérimée addressed to his superiors in the bureaucracy. They are in the form of letters, because established procedures dictated the use of that form. In other jurisdictions, at other times, these reports would have been presented in different forms.

Jean Bonnerot's monumental edition of the Sainte-Beuve correspondence also takes a rigorous view of the question, and excludes almost everything that is not clearly private letters. However, even Bonnerot relents a little and admits into his edition a few texts whose status as letters can be challenged. There is one *draft* of a letter to Victor Hugo, a letter which was written and sent and is now lost. More interesting, because more debatable, there are a few drafts of letters which very possibly were never sent at all.[15] What is the status of a letter which may not have been sent, which in fact may only have been drafted? Is it a letter? No, it is a draft. Should it be included in a published correspondence? Jean Bonnerot thought it should. But he took care to make certain, by means of the annotation, that his reader was aware of the status of the text.[16]

At this point in my investigation, I thought I was beginning to discern a general pattern, according to which even the most conscientious editors of correspondences are occasionally obliged to recognize special cases where a purely arbitrary *ad hoc* decision has to be made about whether a given text is or is not a letter, to be included in a correspondence.

Now the Sainte-Beuve correspondence, like that of Mérimée, was published decades ago (the first volume of the Sainte-Beuve appeared in 1935 and had in fact been ready for publication several years earlier). When we move to more recent editions, such as those of Balzac (begun in 1960, completed in 1969) and of George Sand (begun in 1964, suspended in 1974; soon, we hope, to be continued) we find the editors adopting a much less rigorous approach to the problem of what to include and what to exclude. Balzac's editor, Roger Pierrot, makes a very startling decision at the outset: he will *not* include all of Balzac's letters! He will deliberately exclude one distinct corpus of letters about whose status as letters there can be no doubt, and he will do it for reasons which he presents as mainly practical. He will omit all of the hundreds of letters Balzac wrote to Madame Hanska - letters which are of the greatest literary and historical interest. He does so mainly because the inclusion of these letters would have increased the size of his edition beyond tolerable limits.[17] Now we have a precedent. Not that we believe there is in the Zola correspondence a corpus which in any way resembles the *Lettres à l'Etrangère* (we are practically certain that no such corpus exists);[18] but we have an important decision which has been made on the basis of practical considerations similar to those about which we are concerned for the Zola correspondence. The letters to Madame Hanska are incontestably an integral and important part of Balzac's correspondence. They are omitted, at the cost of considerable inconvenience to readers, for reasons of available space. Practical reasons.

Unhappily our precedent is not quite as clear as we should have liked. Having jettisoned Balzac's supremely important letters to Madame Hanska, allegedly for lack of space, the editor then proceeds to include a considerable number of other items which are not letters. I propose to omit any discussion about the decision to include letters *to* Balzac (or to any of the other writers concerned) in this paper. That is a specific issue, certainly worth discussion; but it is not an issue for the people who are working on the Zola correspondence. We decided at an early stage that we would not include letters to Zola.[19] We have no opinion to express in the present context about other editors' decisions on this question, and I shall not discuss Pierrot's decision to include a large number of letters to Balzac. But what is open to discussion for us, is Pierrot's decision to include also an important number of texts which are simply not letters at all. One accepts easily enough the inclusion of the little classified ads that were Balzac's first replies to Madame Hanska's letters.[20] But one is much more perplexed about the editor's decision to include the texts of contracts that Balzac signed with various publishers.[21] Of course no one would dispute the value of such texts for biographers or historians of the sociology of literature. But one is surprised to find all these texts (and there are a lot of them, because Balzac was always signing contracts, making commitments that he could not and did not honour) inserted in a correspondence exactly as if they were letters; and this, after the decision to exclude all the letters to Madame Hanska.

It has to be said, however, that arguments could be made in defence of the decision to include these non-letters. It was not unusual in the nineteenth century for letters to be considered as having the status of contracts. The Zola correspondence will include some letters in which Zola quite simply writes that he accepts the terms of an agreement he has reached in a conversation with an editor or publisher, and it is clear that for him such a letter has the force of a contract.[22] Now if letters can be contracts, then the distinction between the two categories of text was not as clear in the nineteenth century as it is in the twentieth. (And I am sure that the distinction is far from absolute in our own time). Still I am surprised at the inclusion of such texts within the body of a correspondence, and I am convinced, by an example I shall quote later in this paper, that there are better ways of dealing with them.

Now if the Balzac contracts exist in a kind of interface-area where one cannot be certain about what is and is not suitable material for a correspondence, we are going to discover, as we move on to the George Sand correspondence, some texts which are so steeped in ambiguity that they simply defy any attempt at clear categorization. I don't know whether George Sand's editor has succeeded in making consistent distinctions between letters and non-letters. I don't know whether anybody could. Claude Duchet, in the introduction to his edition of Musset's *Confession d'un enfant du siècle*,[23] writes about a kind of no man's land between literature and lived experience where it becomes impossible to sort out which is which. A lot of the letters which Musset and Sand exchanged are in that ambiguous area. One expects letters to be as close as one can get to an unretouched linguistic representation of lived experience, because they were written in the midst of that experience. But the letters of Musset and Sand were written by persons who were as totally committed to writing as they were to the reality of love and sex. An example: Sand writes to Musset, after the Venetian episode of their liaison and the first separation, that she will be writing him a letter about Venice, but he won't get that letter in the mail; he will read it in the *Revue des deux mondes*. That letter will appear of course in Sand's *Lettres d'un voyageur*,[24] and Georges Lubin will not publish it in the Sand correspondence; but Sand's comment makes it clear that she is simply not interested in making any distinction at all between private letters and public ones. For her, all of her writing is involved in her lived experience, and vice versa. Presumably Musset will read the letter in the *Revue des deux mondes* in a certain way; the general public will read it in another way; the Parisian literati who are curious for spicy details about the Sand-Musset affair will read it in yet another way; and it may even be that Sand is already thinking about posterity.[25] For which reader or group of readers is the text "intended"? It is in cases like these that one is confronted by the real difficulties that are involved in trying to make decisions on the basis of intentions attributed to the writer. We can never hope to decide whether such texts were "intended for publication" or not; we no longer know what that phrase means in relation to such texts.

The result is that, in Lubin's admirable edition of the George Sand correspondence, there are cases where he seems simply to have given up the attempt to make a consistent distinction between texts that are "authentic" letters and texts that are not.[26] Here is what seems to me a clear example of a failure on the editor's part (a failure for which I would never dream of blaming him) to establish and follow a consistent practice: —

Before she became George Sand, Aurore Dudevant wrote, in the winter of 1825 (before she even knew she was a writer!), some pages of a diary. The diary was in the *form* of letters addressed to Aurélien de Sèze, whom she had just seen in Bordeaux after falling in love with him the previous summer. There is no evidence that the texts were ever sent as letters (though it is not impossible that de Sèze may have read them). Lubin publishes these texts as part of the Sand correspondence.[27] Ten years after the letter to de Sèze, the woman who now knows in 1835 that she is George Sand the writer, is in the midst of the most anguished moments of her liaison with Musset, when he, invoking what we call the double standard, has rejected, insulted and abused her because he has learned that she had been to bed with the Venetian doctor before he (Musset) left Venice. She is almost out of her mind with grief and bitterness. She writes down, in a kind of diary, everything she feels. It is among the best things she ever wrote.

There is no doubt that she intended Musset to read that text. There is little doubt that she did give it to him to read, after one of their crazy reconciliations. It is exactly the same kind of intimate journal which she had addressed in 1825 to Aurélien de Sèze. This time, Lubin does not publish it in the correspondence. Instead, he includes it in his edition of Sand's autobiographical writings.[28] He does not say why he made the distinction. One has to presume that the earlier text was included in the correspondence because it had the *form* of letters, and that the later one was excluded because it did not begin with a Dear Alfred or end with a signature. I think that it was an arbitrary decision, and a regrettable one. The two texts are of the same nature, and should be together in the same publication.

But the editor's decision may help us to see further elements of an emerging pattern. The editors of the correspondence of Sainte-Beuve and Mérimée had done their best to stick to a rather rigid set of principles about what does and does not belong in a published correspondence. A few decades later, the editors of the Balzac and Sand correspondences find themselves in possession of some interesting texts which are certainly not letters but which they want to publish, and they make some arbitrary and debatable decisions. In one case, the decision is based primarily on very practical considerations about available space; in another, it is apparently based on the *form* in which the text presents itself. Is there anything to be learned from this?

Going to work on a new edition of the Flaubert correspondence at the beginning of the 1970s, Jean Bruneau gives the impression that there was something to be learned. And I think that the Zola group, which is to begin publishing toward the end of the same decade, can learn something from Bruneau's edition of Flaubert - in spite of the fact that the problems we have to solve are in many ways different from the ones Bruneau faced. As far as the Flaubert correspondence itself is concerned, Bruneau did not have to decide what is a letter and what is not. Flaubert's attitudes to journalism and to the publishing business made it very unlikely that he would ever be caught in the act of writing a letter to the editor, or even a letter-preface. As we know, Flaubert did not lack ideas about literature; but he resisted any desire he may have had to indulge in polemic about his ideas. In that, his case is totally unlike that of Zola, who rarely turned down a chance to discuss his ideas in print. So Flaubert's literary opinions are all expressed in his person-to-person messages, which pose no problems of the kind that concern us.

This is not to say that Bruneau makes no arbitrary decisions. I have yet to find any edition of any correspondence in which the editor was not driven to make *some* arbitrary decisions. Bruneau's decisions concern the choice of letters *to* Flaubert, and as I said above, I do not propose to discuss decisions on that question.[29] The problem which interested me, as I examined the Bruneau edition for possible precedents, concerned texts written *by* an author - texts whose status as letters appeared doubtful, so that one might feel uncertain whether it was appropriate to include them. Bruneau did not have to consider texts whose status as letters was doubtful, but he did have in his possession some texts whose appropriateness in an edition of a correspondence was open to doubt; and this is where he offers a precedent that we can examine. Not all of those texts were letters, though some were; none of them was written by Flaubert; some of them were not even written *to* Flaubert. But all of them contained material directly relevant to the letters published in the first volume of the Flaubert correspondence (I note that we are still waiting for a second volume, as we are still waiting for the rest of the George Sand correspondence - and this waiting reminds us constantly about how precarious are enterprises like ours, and how important the practical considerations can become). In the case of letters *to* Flaubert (from his friends Maxime Du Camp and Alfred Le Poittevin), I confess I don't understand why Bruneau did not include them in the main body of the text, since their status is no more open to doubt than that of the letters from Flaubert's mother or his sister or his mistress, which Bruneau included.

But the texts which are of interest for the present discussion - some pages from Louise Colet's diary, and some letters written to Louise Colet by Maxime Du Camp when he was trying valiantly to be go-between and buffer-state for the passionate and angry lovers - cannot be considered in any way as forming part of Flaubert's correspondence. Still, their relevance is quite unchallengeable. Bruneau decided these texts ought to be published with the correspondence. I do not see how one could argue against him.

Well, as you know if you are familiar with the Bruneau edition, his solution was so luminously, ridiculously simple that one is at first furious with oneself for not having thought of it long ago. He simply puts these texts in appendices at the end of the volume.

We could do something similar in our Zola edition. If we agree that letters intended for publication (or if we want to circumvent the slippery subject of intention, let us just say: published letters) are of a nature different from person-to-person messages, we could put them in appendices at the end of the appropriate volume. But that can only be done if we agree, and at the present time I am not at all certain that we will. (We already have some appendices, and some members of the group may argue against multiplying them.) I feel confident that this will not become a very difficult debate. For myself, I don't much care whether the "doubtful" texts are published in the main body or in appendices; I think the important thing is that we have, in Bruneau's edition of the Flaubert correspondence, a respectable - nay, a prestigious - precedent which (1) justifies the publication of texts whose appropriateness is open to doubt, *and* (2) offers the example of a reasonable procedure for the publication of such texts.

However, let us not rejoice too soon. Bruneau's precedent is by no means without problems. One of the main ones is inconvenience for the reader. I think the convenience of the reader is a very important consideration. If it were the only consideration, or the principal one, then of course editors would simply publish everything in one big edition - letters to, letters from, letters about, letter-prefaces, open letters, pages from diaries, contracts, advertisements, everything. At least that is what the editors would do until the money ran out. The problem is precisely that the money would run out. (It might well be that time also would run out). Our enterprise, like all such enterprises, is precarious. We can't publish everything. We must make decisions about what gets in and what is to be left out.

Bruneau's precedent shows us a form which allows some flexibility, without exposing us to the temptation of trying to publish everything. The main part of the Bruneau edition is composed of texts which are indisputably appropriate because they are person-to-person messages written by or to Flaubert. The appendices are composed of texts which are judged to be important enough to be published even though their appropriateness may be questioned. But this is achieved at the expense of inconvenience to the reader, who may frequently find himself thumbing his way uncomfortably back and forth between the main section and the appendices. That is the price you pay. In the case of Bruneau's edition, it becomes a very heavy price; for Bruneau (or rather, I am sure, Bruneau's publisher, who no doubt insisted on following a procedure that was established long ago for the Pléiade series and has been inconveniencing readers ever since) has multiplied the difficulties in the most irresponsible and absurd way, by putting all the footnotes at the end of the volume, instead of putting them where everybody knows they belong in a correspondence: at the bottom of the page or at the end of the letter. And the inevitable, awful, ridiculous result is that the reader is constantly shuffling back and forth among *four* places in the volume: the main body of the text, the footnotes to it, the appendices, and the footnotes to them. Cruel and unusual punishment for a reader whose only crime is that he wanted to understand.

We certainly won't do that. We'll put our footnotes at the feet. But there will still be some inconvenience to the reader if we decide to adapt Bruneau's precedent to the needs of the Zola correspondence - that is, if we decide that some letters are more, or purer, letters than others. At the present stage of our project, I am inclined to hope that we will decide on this presentation, using an appendix for doubtful cases, with appropriate cross-references to minimize the inconvenience. But I am by no means confident that all of my colleagues on the project will agree. I hope we will decide this way, because the use of an appendix will give us a structure such that we will have to have serious discussion and reflection before we decide to republish texts, such as letter-prefaces and open letters, which were intended for publication and have already been published. It may be that we shall at last decide to publish yet again the famous, admirable, and often-published *J'accuse* - which is, and is not, a letter; but if we follow Bruneau's excellent example, I think we will be confident that we know why we did what we did.[30]

NOTES

1 The team is an international group of researchers who have undertaken to publish a complete annotated edition of all the letters written by Zola which can be found. Ten volumes are planned; the first was published by the University of Montreal Press and the Editions du CNRS in 1978. Bard Bakker (York University, Toronto) is the general editor, and Colette Becker (University of Paris IV) is associate editor. The project operates from offices in the Robarts Research Library, University of Toronto, with the support of the Social Sciences and Humanities Research Council of Canada, the Centre National de Recherche Scientifique, Paris, France, and several Canadian and French universities.

2 Vast-Ricouard, *Vices parisiens: Madame Bécart*, Paris, Derveaux, 1879.

3 The letter appeared in *Le Figaro*, 6 September 1880; it is included in the Mitterand edition of the *Oeuvres complètes*, XIV, Paris, Cercle du Livre Précieux, 1970, p. 1,410.

4 The first newspaper publication was in *L'Aurore*, 13 January 1898. In the following days, several Parisian newspapers published the text in whole or in part. The article first appeared in book form in Emile Zola, *La Vérité en marche*, Paris, Charpentier, 1901; it is included in the Mitterand edition of the *Oeuvres complètes*, XIV, Paris, Cercle du Livre Précieux, 1970, pp. 921-31.

5 Mitterand was, with Pierre Robert (then Chairman of the Department of French, University College, University of Toronto), a founding father of the Zola Research Programme and the principal instigator of the correspondence project.

6 Zola, *Correspondance*, I, Presses de l'Université de Montréal, 1978, pp. 14-15.

7 Sainte-Beuve, *Correspondance générale*, Paris, Stock, later Privat-Didier, 1935-75, 17 vols. to date.

8 Prosper Mérimée, *Correspondance générale*, Paris, Le Divan, 1941-64, 17 vols.

9 Balzac, *Correspondance* (Classiques Garnier), Paris, Garnier, 1960-69, 5 vols.

10 George Sand, *Correspondance* (1812-52), (Classiques Garnier), Paris, Garnier, 1964-74, 10 vols. to date.

11 Flaubert, *Correspondance*, I (1830-51), Paris, Gallimard, Bibliothèque de la Pléiade, 1973.

12 In this connection, one particular field seems to me to be crying out for investigation. We all know about the double standard concerning love and sex which existed in western society in the nineteenth century, and continues to exist in the twentieth. We all know about it, but we don't know all about it. Reading the letters of George Sand to Musset, and those of Flaubert to Louise Colet, I realized how much we can learn, and should learn, from these correspondences about the enormous psychic damage that was inflicted principally on women, but also on men, by the double standard. There is an important book to be written about that. We already have a title for it: a phrase written by one of the victims of the double standard, Louise Colet. Returning home after an agonizing encounter with Flaubert, wracked with anguish and anger, she scribbled these words in her journal: "Humiliation de la femme dans l'amour" (published in the Flaubert *Correspondance*, I, p. 813: see note 11). When that book is written, the great correspondences of the nineteenth-century writers will be among the principal sources of documentation.

13 It may be that material considerations also played a part. The Mérimée correspondence began to be published in 1941, shortly after the beginning of the German occupation of Paris. Paper was scarce, and the editor may have been obliged to omit texts of a kind that will appear later in other correspondences, as will be

shown in this paper.

14 Women were an important part of these pleasures, as Mérimée's letters make very clear. His correspondence is a mine of documentation for the study of women as sex objects in the nineteenth century.

15 Sainte-Beuve, *Correspondance générale*, I, Paris, Stock, 1935, pp. 281-82.

16 *Ibid.*, p. 283, n. 1.

17 See Pierrot's Introduction to Balzac, *Correspondance*, I, Paris, Garnier, 1960, p. XII.

18 There are some letters written by Zola to Jeanne Rozerot, the mother of his two children; however these letters are in no way comparable, in number or in importance, to the *Lettres à l'Etrangère*.

19 There were various reasons, but the main one was that we would have had more than 14,000 letters to publish, instead of about 4,000.

20 Balzac, *Correspondance*, I, 1960, p. 187 and II, 1962, pp. 189-90.

21 *Ibid.*, I, pp. 197, 220, 256, 257, 281, 282, 283, 286, 290, etc.

22 An example: Zola's letter to Jules Laffitte, 10 May 1879 (published in the Bernouard edition of the Zola correspondence, II, 1928, p. 527).

23 The Classiques Garnier edition, Paris, 1968, p. III.

24 In George Sand, *Oeuvres autobiographiques* II, Paris, Gallimard, Bibliothèque de la Pléiade, 1971, pp. 653-78. The two following letters (*ibid.*, pp. 679-735) are also addressed to Musset. The letters first appeared in the *Revue des deux mondes*, 15 May 1834, 15 July 1834, 15 September 1834.

25 See the following note for further evidence of Sand's concern for posterity.

26 I am not referring here to the spectacular case of the letters which Sand, with magnificent perfidy, simply revised twenty years after the event, and then tucked back into her collection of letters, never dreaming that she would be caught at it more than a century later by her editor's equally magnificent detective work (see Lubin's edition of Sand, *Correspondance*, II, Paris, Garnier, 1964,

pp. 538-41).

27 *Ibid.*, I, pp. 175-259.

28 George Sand, *Journal intime*, in *Oeuvres autobiographiques*, Paris, Gallimard, Bibliothèque de la Pléiade, 1971, pp. 953-71.

29 Personally, I am very grateful to Bruneau for including the letters Caroline Flaubert wrote to her brother Gustave, in addition to his letters to her. One cannot help feeling a little less pessimistic about the human race after one has read the evidence of the unfailing tenderness, generosity, and good humour that characterized the relations between Caroline and Gustave Flaubert. It was too good to last. Caroline was not yet 22 when she died of complications resulting from childbirth. Flaubert transferred his love to her daughter, and later her daughter's husband ruined him. But that is biographical anecdote. The letters that Caroline and Gustave Flaubert exchanged are a moral lesson. Bruneau's arbitrary decision to include them in the Flaubert correspondence was right, beyond all argument. It would have been a crime against humanity to leave them out. They ought to be required reading in courses about family relationships.

30 The problem with which this paper deals did not have to be settled before the publication of the first volume of the Zola correspondence. No "doubtful" texts appeared in the period (1858-67) covered by the first volume - a further indication that the cases discussed are indeed special. A decision will be needed for the second volume, however; and at the present stage of our discussions it seems unlikely that we shall follow the Bruneau model. The working group appears to favour a solution which divides both the letter-prefaces and the open letters into sub-categories. Some of the letter-prefaces which Zola wrote for publication were subsequently collected by him and published in book form; consequently they have already appeared in the Mitterand edition of the *Oeuvres complètes* (Paris, Cercle du Livre Précieux, 1966-70, 15 vols.) These letter-prefaces will not appear in the correspondence; all other letter-prefaces (including the one to Vast and Ricouard, mentioned at the beginning of the paper) will be published. In the

case of open letters, a similar criterion will be used. Those which Zola himself gathered and published in book form will be excluded, while those which until now have only been published in newspapers will appear in the correspondence. (Since the text of *J'accuse* has been published many times, it would be excluded on the basis of this criterion).

Members of the Conference

Margaret Anderson, *University of Toronto*
John D. Baird, *University of Toronto*
B.H. Bakker, *Glendon College, York University*
R.A. Barrell, *University of Guelph*
Alan Bell, *National Library of Scotland*
Virginia Bemis, *Michigan State University*
G.E. Bentley, Jr., *University of Toronto*
Cicely Blackstock, *University of Toronto*
Kenneth Blackwell, *McMaster University*
William F. Blissett, *University of Toronto*
Edward A. Bloom, *Brown University*
Lillian D. Bloom, *Rhode Island College*
Nicole Boursier, *University of Toronto*
Kristin M. Brady, *University of Toronto*
Andrew Brink, *McMaster University*
Angus Cameron, *University of Toronto*

Michael T. Cartwright, *McGill University*
Michael Collie, *York University*
Don L. Cook, *Indiana University*
George B. Cooper, *Trinity College, Hartford*
Judith Curtis, *Scarborough College*
J.A. Dainard, *University of Toronto*
H.B. de Groot, *University of Toronto*
A.H. de Quehen, *University of Toronto*
Eric Domville, *University of Toronto*
Robert Finch, *University of Toronto*
Esther Safer Fisher, *University of Toronto*
P.G. Gardner, *Memorial University of Newfoundland*
Hilda Gifford, *Carleton University*
Harry Girling, *York University*
Joseph Gold, *University of Waterloo*
Victor E. Graham, *University of Toronto*
Rachel K. Grover, *University of Toronto*
Francess G. Halpenny, *University of Toronto*
Mihai H. Handrea, *The Carl H. Pforzheimer Library*
Patricia Hernlund, *Wayne State University*
Emita B. Hill, *Herbert H. Lehman College, City University of New York*
Kayla Hoffman, *Social Sciences and Humanities Research Council of Canada*
G.A. Hollingshead, *University of Alberta*
J.R. de J. Jackson, *University of Toronto*
Jean C. Jamieson, *University of Toronto Press*
Eugène Joliat, *University of Toronto*
James King, *McMaster University*
Slava Klima, *McGill University*
Richard G. Landon, *University of Toronto*
Paul LeClerc, *Union College, Schenectady*
Ralph A. Leigh, *Trinity College, Cambridge*
John W. Lennox, *York University*
Wilmarth S. Lewis, *The Lewis Walpole Library, Farmington*

Emile Lizé, *University of Ottawa*
Michael McCarthy, *University of Toronto*
Norman Mackenzie, *Ryerson Polytechnical Institute*
Hugh MacLean, *State University of New York, Albany*
Kenneth MacLean, *University of Toronto*
Charlotte W. Mangold, *Pennsylvania State University, Ogontz Campus*
Edwin W. Marrs, Jr., *University of Pittsburgh*
Paul F. Mattheisen, *State University of New York, Binghamton*
John Matthews, *Queen's University*
Barbara Meadowcroft, *McGill University*
J.W.R. Meadowcroft, *Concordia University*
James A.C. Means, *Université Laval*
J.L. Mercié, *University of Ottawa*
Jane Millgate, *University of Toronto*
Michael Millgate, *University of Toronto*
George Monteiro, *Brown University*
Peter F. Morgan, *University of Toronto*
R. Gordon Moyles, *University of Alberta*
Brenda Murphy, *St. Lawrence University*
Eugene F. Murphy, *Hobart and William Smith Colleges*
Irena Murray, *McGill University*
Charles Anthony Myrans, *Yale University*
Desmond Neill, *University of Toronto*
Victor A. Neufeldt, *University of Victoria*
Fergal Nolan, *University of Toronto*
David J. Nordloh, *Indiana University*
Sybille Pantazzi, *Art Gallery of Ontario*
Roger Peattie, *University of Calgary*
Thomas Pinney, *Pomona College*
John C. Riely, *Yale University*
César Rouben, *McMaster University*
William Rueter, *University of Toronto Press*
James B. Sanders, *University of Western Ontario*

D.A. Signori, *University of Toronto*
D.I.B. Smith, *University of Auckland*
D.W. Smith, *University of Toronto*
Dorothy E. Speirs, *University of Toronto*
Richard Switzer, *California State College, San Bernardino*
Clara Thomas, *York University*
Clive Thomson, *Queen's University*
Prudence Tracy, *University of Toronto Press*
Lars Troide, *McGill University*
Charles Vandersee, *University of Virginia*
Miriam Waddington, *York University*
John A. Walker, *University of Toronto*
Catherine Coogan Ward, *Western Kentucky University*
Robert E. Ward, *Western Kentucky University*
Sister Martha Westwater, *Mount St. Vincent University*
Thomas Woodson, *Ohio State University*
Arthur C. Young, *Russell Sage College*
G.J. Zytaruk, *Nipissing University College*

Index